Quiet Retreat Teachings

Book III: Second Sight

Diamond Mountain University Press

dmu-press.com

More by Geshe Michael Roach:

The Principal Teachings of Buddhism (author Je Tsongkapa, compiler Geshe Michael Roach)

Preparing for Tantra: The Mountain of Blessings (authors Je Tsong-kapa, Geshe Michael Roach, Lobsang Tharchin)

The Diamond Cutter:
The Buddha on Managing Your Business and Your Life

The Garden: A Parable

How Yoga Works: Healing Yourself and Others with the Yoga Sutra

The Essential Yoga Sutra: Ancient Wisdom for Your Yoga

The Tibetan Book of Yoga:
Ancient Buddhist Teachings on the Philosophy and Practice of Yoga

The Eastern Path to Heaven:
A Guide to Happiness from the Teachings of Jesus in Tibet

Karmic Management:
 What Goes Around Comes Around in Your Business and Your Life

Quiet Retreat Teachings

Second Sight

by Geshe Michael Roach

September 20 - 23, 2001
Diamond Mountain Retreat Center

St. David, Arizona

Diamond Mountain University Press

dmu-press.com

Diamond Mountain University Press
dmu-press.com

Second Sight
Quiet Retreat Teachings
Book 3

Published in the United States by Diamond Mountain University Press
Visit our website at www.dmu-press.com

ISBN-10: 0-9837478-3-0

PRINTED IN THE UNITED STATES OF AMERICA

Book Design and Cover by Katey Fetchenhier

2 0 1 1 0 7 0 0 0 1

Table of Contents

Preface

I.5-6 The mind turns in five different ways.
They can be involved with afflictions or free of them.
The five are correct perceptions,
mistaken perceptions, imagination, sleep, and memories.

Virttayah panchatayyah klishta-aklishtah.
`Pramana viparyaya vikalpa nidra smirtayah.

I.7 The different types of correct perception
are those which are direct;
deductive; or based on authority.

Pratyaksha-anumana-agamah pramanani.

-Master Patanjali, Yoga Sutra

Between March 3, 2000 and June 6, 2003, Geshe Michael Roach and several of his senior students engaged in a three-year silent meditation retreat in the desert wilderness of southeastern Arizona. During that time he didn't see anyone apart from the six retreatants, didn't get any news from the outside world, and didn't even hear the sound of a human voice. However, in order to fulfill a promise he had made to his students before he left, Geshe Michael came blindfolded to the edge of the retreat boundary twice a year to teach, and students came from Australia, Ireland, England, Germany, Mongolia, Singapore and throughout the United States to listen to these teachings.

It was Sept. 20th, 2001, the nineteenth month of the three-year retreat. Many flights were grounded, and people were afraid to take even the ones that were in operation, for fear that they may be hijacked or worse. The students came by train or bus or car, huddling together in the desert, exchanging stories of how it had happened for them, crying together, asking after friends who may have been at the Trade Center when it fell. The New Yorkers were shell shocked, some telling horror stories: of being trapped for hours in the dark, separated from loved ones with no way of knowing if they were alive or dead, hearing the screams or seeing the bodies fall, how the smell of death that lingered all over the city. Some were speechless, still unable to articulate what they had experienced; some just held each other and cried. They came because they were drawn to the only comfort and refuge that made any sense anymore, the teacher who had helped them to make sense of the suffering of our lives.

These are the teachings given at that time by one of the only people in the world who didn't know about the tragedy of 9-11. He quotes from the Yoga Sutra to explain how we perceive and misperceive our world. He talks about how to derive comfort from beings you can't see or haven't met yet, or from the enlightened being you will become. He gives hints about how to connect with the masters of the past, by taking their teachings into our hearts. Finally he explains how the world we think we see is an impossibility. And how to create a world with no barriers, where everyone is close.

So as you read, imagine you are sitting with these friends in the wake of 9-11, listening to your teacher, your old friend, as he tries to pass on something that will be of give meaning to your life. The moment is precious; he has only a short time to tell you everything he wants you to know, and then he will go back for another six months of quiet, and you will go back to a world that so desperately needs this wisdom.

At the beginning of each evening's teaching is a short verse, or you could say a root text, around which the teaching would be formed. You can use these verses later to contemplate the thoughts behind them, try to make them your own and use them to help others. This is what these teachings are for and that is what this book is for.

These books are transcripts of those Arizona desert Quiet Retreat Teachings. It is incredibly rare to receive teachings from a Teacher immersed in deep retreat, and our intention is to share the special wisdom and blessings of these unique teachings with you. We have kept editing to a minimum in order to preserve the freshness of Geshe Michael's language and the several layers of meaning they sometimes convey.

First Day:

Thursday, September 20, 2001

I.

We can see the sky.
Blue, lit from within;
Better than any sapphire.

We can see the stars,
Fire itself,
Beyond any diamond.

We can see the mountains
And hold the warmth of earth in our hands.

We can see life,
Sparks of intelligence and kindness:
We can see each other.

Down our streets we can see
Schools, hospitals,
Homes for the elderly,

Churches and people of every kind;
Peace,
Striving to reach and touch -

This precious, present moment.

A pinpoint
On an unseen plain
That knows no horizon.

A pinpoint
In an unseen river
That stretches forever.

It is
Too much not to see.
It is
Where have we come from?
What will become of us?
What have we come here to do?

It is
All the only things
That matter.

To see
You have to have a reason
To see; it is
The one thing left unseen
Because we do not want
To see it.

Children of the rabbit
In the dark of a thousand
Miles of empty desert,

Caught in the jaws of the serpent;

Who will help us?

You know us.

For better or worse,
We have worked
Side by side.

You see our houses;
You know where we live,
You know what we try to do.

So how can you leave us
Clawing at the dirt?
How can you leave us here?

I haven't spoken for a long time, and if I have trouble then Winston is here to help.

Then, for all of us in retreat, on behalf of everyone in retreat, I'd like to thank you for coming here. It's a great blessing for us, and we feel really happy because we can feel you even as you are planning to come. It gets very loud [laughter], and some of our teachers are here and we're very lucky to have you here.

I think we could meditate for a few minutes first. OK, we'll start.

There's a story in my family, and I think it's true. Our grandfather—his name was Horatio Sawyer Earle—he had a business in the city where he lived. He made tools and machines, and in the same city there was another tool company that was founded by my other grandfather, and that was called the Andrew Company. I think they were competitors.

One day a man, a young man, came to see my grandfather, grandfather Earle, and he was asking for help. He wanted to start a new kind of business, and my grandfather Earle said, "Well, what is it you want to do?"

3

And the young man said, "I want to make things, a certain thing that almost no one has ever seen."

My grandfather said, "Is that all?"

And then he said, "No, I want to make it in a new way that no one has ever tried."

Then grandfather said, "Is that all?"

And he said, "No. The third thing, this thing is going to cost almost a years pay of a person, and I think everyone will want one."

My grandfather said, "You want to make something that no one has seen much at all. You expect to make it in a new way, and you expect everyone to put out a years salary to get one, and you think everyone will get one?"

And he said, "That's right."

Then grandfather Earle said, "You're crazy," and he sent him away without a penny.

And then Henry Ford went to other people in Detroit and started the Ford Motor Company. The people in my family, we figure we lost about five hundred million dollars. I think it's true.

Being in retreat is the same. We came to people and said, "Will you help us? We want to try something; we want to try to reach something that no one has really seen much, especially in this country. We hope that it will be mass-produced later. We hope that everyone could have it in their garage or home, or in their heart and mind."

And so we tried to find people who would believe in something they couldn't even see and almost no one had ever seen. And you are those people. We know that most of the people helping us are here. We know there's not that many. We know [crying] your sacrifice, some of you much of your life, and some of you almost everything you had to help us. We know we're not cheap like the old yogis in Tibet. We know it's hard.

4

We can hear it when the holy caretakers are struggling on a day. They came on the hottest days of the year. I think it was hundred and ten, hundred and fifteen. They worked, we could hear them making things for us, and every day cooking, every day trying to find people to help, every day bringing us things, magically they just show up. All for something no one can see.

And there are many people like them. We have teachers coming. Holy teachers come to help us learn ways to meditate better, take care of ourselves. People have sent beautiful things for our altars, offerings, precious books, and all for something you can't see.

And the retreatants here have worked very, very hard. They feel the pressure of others serving them. They are afraid to waste a minute. They never stop working, all day, all week, and it's all for something that no one can even see, something that very few people have ever seen. They are trying to reach it, to help others.

Then you're all very special people. You're very rare among the people in the world to commit your life to try to reach something that no one has seen much, to commit your life and time, and your money, and your family, to help others reach something that no one has really seen. You're very special, all of you. We are very lucky to be together.

I used to work in the diamond business. There's a building called Five-Eighty-Fifth. It's on the corner of Fifth Avenue and 47th. It's about, I think, forty stories high. It's a huge building. It has hundreds and hundreds of offices, and all of them deal in diamonds and other precious stones. I think almost three quarters of the several billion dollars of diamonds that enter this country every year come through those offices.

I can remember we would go there, to an office high up in the sky, and the sky would be there, on the Eastern side, beautiful sky, and we would sit down and start a diamond deal. It's a lot of screaming and arguing, and all sorts of pleading. It's kind of fun, and exhausting. Sometimes a big deal would go on for days. We would come back day after day. Then finally, *"Mazal. Mazal u'bracha.* I give my sacred word of honor to keep this deal."

There are no papers. There are no contracts. Millions of dollars of diamonds have been dealt on a handshake. There are no lawyers allowed to deal in the diamond club because there are no disagreements.

Then afterwards everyone would relax back in their chairs exhausted and happy, each side thinking they had gotten a better deal. And you would drink something together and feel like family. The Brazilians would pull out this thick coffee with more sugar in it. The Chinese would pull out this wonderful jasmine tea. The Israelis would pull out a diet Coke.

And then the owner would lean back towards his vault, his safe, and he would say quietly, "I have an important stone." In the trade "important stone" means a major stone. It could be a diamond of several hundred carats, something that few people have ever seen.

I remember an Indian dealer. He opened his safe. There's a quiet that descends on the room. He took out a white velvet box and he opened it, and we all clustered around silently. It was a huge Kashmir sapphire, I think sixty carats or more, and it's almost priceless.

Then I remember looking out the window at the sky, and I thought, honestly, the sky is more beautiful than this stone. It's a beautiful stone, but the sky has its own light. The sky is blue with its own light, and it's free. All of us can see the sky. It's so beautiful. I think if you spend a lot of time maybe meditating or maybe in a prison or maybe if you're about to die and you know it, the sky becomes a very precious thing—rare, precious, free for everyone, beautiful blue azure.

The stars are the same. This teaching is being held towards the new moon. You will be able to see unbelievable stars. In Antwerp, Belgium we used to sit with really beautiful Jain dealers. One of them took me to his special room. There were sacks of raw diamonds piled everywhere. Huge sacks of diamonds, and I looked at them. It was evening, and his office faced the North sky. It was dark and there were beautiful stars. I thought the stars were more beautiful, each with a little color, each with their own fire.

We are very fortunate, we are very lucky. We are surrounded by intense beauty. The mountain that you see in front of you, as the sun goes down, turns beautiful crimson red. It's so beautiful to watch after a hard day. We can see these things free—the sky, stars, mountain, sun. The ground you're sitting on is a kind of special gravel from millions of years of the once-a-year flood. And when you touch it you can feel the warmth that came from the sun. It's such a wonderful thing to hold the earth in your hands

In Mongolia in the countryside, in the torn-down ruined hermitages of the Buddhist meditators, you can still find a person or two, they will share what they have with you. And then after you've eaten they will take a big, smooth stone from the hearth, and they will say, "Hold it." And it's dessert to just hold the earth and feel the warmth of fire, and it calms the heart.

We can see all of these things. They are free. And around us here the trees, especially the old oaks, they are teeming with life. Sometimes I imagine them like New York apartment buildings, huge towers, and on the top floors are all the blue jays, crows, sparrows, each with his own song. Little lower are all the crawling things, praying mantises, lizards. A little lower are all the squirrel homes and there are also holes for beautiful mice, different kinds, and then the majestic snakes which eat them. But they are full of life; they don't look like it.

And when you've been alone or meditating a long time it's very precious to see life. They are not stupid. They have sparks of intelligence, kindness. If you've lived with the small creatures a long time you start to see how they take care of each other. The small sparrows, no bigger than your hand, they will come to eat the cookies you send us, and if they find a nice piece they will run to the other sparrow and give it to them, into their mouth. And you can hear their beautiful voices like a stream singing, "Thank you," to each other. The blue jays crowd around the water dish that we've set out, and with great dignity and respect for each other, the eldest go first and drink, and the others will stand and wait. It's beautiful to see.

Even the mother cows here, if you approach a group of them, the father will come forth and challenge you. He will protect his wife cow and children, and the mother cow will take the children back away to a safe distance. They are like families. They cry for each other when they get separated. The young ones love their parents, they hug them.

Even the ants, if they find another ant dead, will, it seems, respectfully pick up the body and carry it to the side and set it down, it seems with great compassion.

We can see these precious things all around us. You drive down any street of a city or town in this country. You can see schools, beautiful large schools, with beautiful large places for the children to play. Free schools for children. This is a very precious thing. This has not existed in this world in the past. We are very lucky. Before only wealthy people's children could have a book, could learn. We are living in special times.

You can see hospitals. This is unheard of in the violent history of our kind. Free care for poor people who need it. A place where anyone can go, with a little red tape, and get care for their sickness. In the whole history of mankind this is special. The sick were ignored or left to die unless they had close family.

You can see special homes for elderly. They are not perfect. Sometimes they are dirty, noisy, crazy, but in the history of man on this planet, no one has taken care of old people like we try to.

If you drive down any street you can see different churches, temples, mosques, and everyone free to go where they like. Everyone free to worship, to try to reach their own god. No one torturing you, beating you. No one demanding that you follow their god. This is totally new in this planet. We can see these things. We are unbelievably fortunate.

We can walk down streets of a city like New York and see twenty, thirty, forty different countries' peoples working together, taking care of each other, living in relative peace. This is unheard of in this world. We take it for granted. It has never been that way.

We have lived in peace. This particular country hasn't really been attacked in a hundred years. Our children don't know what it means to hide from a bomb coming down, or what it means to be killed or raped by soldiers coming through your town. This is new in this world.

We are incredibly blessed. We can see all of these precious things, from the sky to each other. Each person here, precious, like a snowflake, each one with her or his own special skills, their own feelings, their own devotions. We can see the most amazing thing: it's each other. We can see all of these things in this one moment, in this one holy moment that we travel in, the present moment. We can enjoy all of these extraordinary, beautiful things.

But if you think about it, we live only in a moment. We travel around in a single instant of time. We are confined to a single instant, a single moment. We can only see these precious things in the present moment. Time goes ahead of us like a river. Time goes behind us like a river. There's no end in either direction, and we are confined to a moment. We can only see the moment we're in.

The places where living beings live are infinite. They stretch out from the spot you are in, in all directions, countless worlds, countless realms. We can't even see a few of them. We are confined to a few yards of space. We can only see what's around us.

Those things we see are precious, yes, but the things we can't see, worlds in the space around us, countless worlds, countless people striving, living, struggling on those worlds, beings we can't imagine that run in the same place where you sit. We are surrounded by infinite places and wonderful creatures of different kinds. We can't even see them. We are stuck in a small few yards. It's too much. We are like a single point on a needle, and there's infinite time ahead. We can't see any of it.

I saw a retreatant. She was walking. She looked at her foot. She froze. I thought, "What's wrong?" I looked down. There was a large snake, poisonous, curled under her foot. Why can't we see just a minute ahead? Why are we confined to a single moment? How many of you have been in an accident, hurt yourself badly, seen people die, because we can't see one minute ahead into infinite time ahead of us? We are handicapped. We are crippled. The present moment is nothing.

We have no idea where we came from—be honest. People have different philosophies. They all exist because no one knows. You don't know where you were a few minutes before you came into this world. You're not even sure if you were anywhere. Can't see back. Don't know how we came here. Even while we're here we don't know why we came here. Be honest. Why is all this here? Why is the world like this? What are we supposed to be doing here? Who sent us? What are we really meant to do? We don't really know.

And think of all the people who died not knowing. You know them. You've had friends, family. They have died, but where did they go? We have no idea. You have philosophies, religions, you have people guessing. Can't see.

We can see the sky. We can see the stars, and we can touch the ground, and we are locked in this tiny moment of time, and the only things that matter. Where did we come from? Why are we here? What are we supposed to do? Where did our loved ones go? Where are we going? We can't see any of the things that really matter. We are blind to the only things that matter.

So I would like in these four short days to talk about how to see these things yourself. How can you see what's going to happen to you in the long run? How can you learn to see? Because you can. You can see precisely, and directly, what you will be, and I'd like to talk about learning to see all the places you are, because you can.

The human mind has this capacity. You can see countless realms. You can see every living creature living on those worlds, and you can see all that in a single moment, as you see this desert and sky now. You have the capacity.

You can meet holy, divine creatures, beings who live around you now, directly. You can see higher reality than this. There is a higher one. This is a very ordinary and plain reality. The moment that we are locked into. There is a divine reality. There is a higher one. You can go there. You can see it. You can be part of it. You have the capacity. I would like to talk about how to do it.

But first you have to experience refreshments *[laughs]*. So please enjoy it, don't be shy, and enjoy it. People have worked hard to serve you, and enjoy it, thank them, and we'll start again after that, when Winston makes some noise.

[Break]

We talked about things that we can't see. We can't see even a few seconds or minutes into a future which goes forever. We can't see more than a few yards around us, of worlds upon worlds. There are divine beings around us constantly. We can't see any of them. They're in a higher kind of reality than the one we are in. It's around us all the time. We can't see it. It's because we don't have the capacity. We haven't developed our true capacity.

But there's one thing we don't see because we don't want to see. I think it's ironic that this is the only thing that can help us to see the other things. So if you truly want to learn, and you can, to see all those things, you have to have a good reason to see them. You have to want to see, in your heart, to see them, so deeply you may not even know it. So you have to learn to see the thing that we don't like to see,

10

and then it will come in your heart, a strong, burning desire, drive it takes to see all those things, and then you will be able to see them.

If you don't see this one thing, you will never see the other. You won't even think it's possible. You won't even, maybe, care.

People in long retreats like to complain to each other by hand signs that nothing's happening. In the next minute they tell you a story like this. One of the retreatants, a holy person, kind person, was doing her prayers, quietly. Then meditating, and then she could hear something, a small, tiny, tiny squeaking thing outside. And then there was an act of a bodhisattva. She moved, she moved up off her seat. There's a holy, golden moment in the time of a person's life. She went to see who is crying.

Not far from her yurt she saw a baby rabbit, child rabbit. They are very beautiful. They are only as big as your hand. They are innocent. They move very slow. They don't know it's dangerous. They're soft, warm. They don't run away from you. They are like Twinkies in the desert for other creatures, and this one was already half way down the jaws of a huge snake, and it was crying.

For what do you cry? You are living in a thousand miles of empty desert. It's almost dark. A huge snake has you in its jaws, powerful jaws. These snakes are about as big around as the bottom of one of our legs. Why should the baby cry? It's hopeless. Why should the child cry in the dark, in a huge empty desert? There isn't a creature around large enough to help who won't eat it also, but the baby was crying.

Then this kind woman who claims nothing is happening in her retreat instantly ran and confronted the snake. This is a second act of a bodhisattva. And because of the power of her, the snake backed off, just like that—no weapons—and the child was left on the ground, crawling in the dirt, and one of its legs was half eaten off *[crying]*. And so she nursed it. Now it's a big fat baby. I think you can see it in the caretakers' place. When he runs he clicks on the bone of his destroyed leg.

And sometimes I sit, I can't help thinking about him, half way down the mouth of a huge snake, crying in the dark in an empty desert. Why should the child cry? I can't stop wondering. And then you think of the baby. You look down at the small rabbit. How sad, how pitiful, how hopeless to cry. Just die.

11

I can't stop thinking that we are the same. Every time I think of the child rabbit I can't stop thinking that we are all the same. We aren't stronger than that child. We aren't really much bigger. We can't control what happens to us. We've seen the people we love die, torn away in an instant. We save baby rabbits and we don't stop to think we are the same. We aren't more powerful than that baby child. We are half way down the mouth of the lord of death. There isn't a person who isn't halfway down. There isn't a single person here who isn't half dead already. We don't cry because we know it won't help. It's not normal to cry out loud all day among other people, but inside somewhere, you know that it's true. You and I and every other person here is half way down those jaws. Sometimes now when I see people I can't help seeing jaws around their legs, half way up their thighs. I can't help thinking, "Who will be the next one?"

We've all been together. We are together now. You know the other people here, or most of them. You like some of them, maybe some not so much. You know where we live. You can see our yurts. You can see the tops, I think. You know we go there. You know we really try hard to do our prayers. We really try hard to do something that will help, but we aren't much stronger than that little rabbit. We are halfway dead already. You can't just leave this place knowing that the person who lives in one yurt will die first, and then the second. You will find out from a friend, "You know the Diamond Mountain retreat people? One of them died today."

Then there'll be another. You don't want to think about it. It's hard to look around, the people around you right now. It's hard to know. We are all half dead. There's almost no hope. We are really trying hard. It's a very hard thing to do. You have to help us.

I will curse you with a thought now until tomorrow. Every time you see someone, you see them halfway down the open jaws, and the jaws are clamped on them. Who is going to save anyone? Try to see the jaws tonight, tomorrow. Every time you look at another of the holy, sweet, precious, fragile beings who are with you, try to remember. Try to see what's really going on. Some of us seem strong, some seem weaker, some seem older, some younger, some happier, some more sad. We're all dying. We're all halfway down. It's very hard to change. It's very hard to help, but you have to try.

You can't just leave us, she didn't just leave the rabbit. Later she was bitten by a snake trying to help. She spent two days in the hospital. Other retreatants have

12

done the same thing. You have to try. This is the reason to learn to see more things. You have to save us. "Oh, I'm just visiting." *[Laughs.]* You are the ones in retreat now. You have to save us. We've tried. It's hard.

Each person—and this is the nature of things—has to save the others. It's always like that. *You* have to save *us*. You can't do it unless you can see the future. You can't do it unless you can see how many of us there are. You can't do it if you can't even see our world. You can't do it without the help of the divine, holy, sweet, perfect beings who are hovering around us constantly. You can't do it without seeing higher reality, and your past.

But if you learn how, you can. You can pull us out of the jaws of death. It's not too late for anyone here.

"I never heard of a person who didn't have to die." Don't be like grandfather Earle. This is a special time. These are special circumstances. There are special events happening here. There's special knowledge. There's a special path. People have been on it. You can learn to do it, but in your heart you have to have a strong reason, because it's hard to do. If you don't have that reason there's no hope for you, and there's no hope for all of us who are hoping you can help us.

Whenever it's hard, whenever you think you're not making any progress, whenever the world is too strong, too much, the demands on your life are too insistent, your body getting older; your mind hardly strong enough to stay on an even keel, then remember the baby. Think of that child. Get up off your seat. Go see how you can help. This will give you the strength you need. Then you can do anything. You can see anything.

Second Day:

Friday, September 21, 2001

II.

Stumbling to our graves
In boxes
A little bigger than ourselves;
Cloaked in four silver curtains
At the edge of what we see.

Ahead, what we will be;
Behind, what we were.

On the right side
Endless worlds
And the hearts of those who wait
In pain and hope for us.

On the left,
Beings of the divine,
Themselves a higher truth.

Draw them to you;
Call them first
From the dark world of *Viparyaya*,
The realm of cannot be.

Next through the mists
Of the ocean of *Vikalpa*,
Place of the maybe could.

14

And then the first great leap,

To the sturdy shores of *Agama*,
First land of it is,
A deeply hidden is,
For spoken it was so.

Closer, to the highlands
Of *Anumana*:
The simply hidden is,
At reason's true demand.

Then lastly to the sunlit peaks
Of the mountains of *Pratyaksha*
Second great leap, the undeniable power
Of something in your hand.

To remember,
Think of the vegetables,
And remember reaching out to touch.
Their hands just there, to the right.

So meditate for a few minutes... OK, we'll start.

Sometimes you don't see a friend of yours for maybe a few years, and then the next time you next see them they look much older, but if you stay with the same person from day to day, you don't notice it. And I think it's even harder to notice the changes in yourself, because you're always with yourself. So especially for people who are trying to work mighty changes in themselves, it can be frustrating because you're with yourself all the time. You sometimes don't notice how much you've changed, and then it's easy to get discouraged. So I thought it would be good to say a little about where you are from the viewpoint of a person who is watching you.

There are unfortunate people in the world who don't have enough money or food.

And then there is the great medium middle class, the people who have enough—not a lot—but if they didn't have that, they wouldn't be alive, so they do have that. Then among those, a few thousand people, there will be one or two who rise to great wealth, and among those, even a few people we can say are so wealthy they don't even know exactly how much they have anymore. In the diamond business, we would meet people like that. They were so wealthy they lost track of their wealth. They couldn't even remember how many houses they had.

But in the Abhidharma and other texts, there's an idea—I think you could translate it as leapfrogging—like jumping over something by intense karma, intense wishes and devotion. And you can go from a normal medium person financially, and you can leapfrog over all the wealthy and super wealthy and beyond wealthy. You become an even more exclusive person who doesn't even notice what they have. They have contentment; in Sanskrit, santosha. They are just happy. They don't remember how much money they have or don't have. Maybe they have a lot, maybe they don't have any, but they're happy. And that's more rare than the very wealthy. And the people, especially the holy caretakers and other staff and director here and the people in retreat—you should know; you should be proud and happy, because you have leapfrogged over wealthy and super wealthy. And I'm not being poetic or metaphorical or sour grapes. It's really true. You've gone in a short few years beyond super wealthy. There are only a few fortunate people on this planet who have reached the state of wealth that you have. You should know it; you should appreciate how far you've gone.

And I think it's important to say never look back at the very wealthy or the wealthy or the well-off people with so-called security, because there is none. You have found the real security. So don't ever look back; try to stay where you've come to.

The same applies to your home. Most of us had lived in small but nice places: some of us had a house; others had apartments. And we've now leapfrogged over people who have beautiful large houses to the satisfaction of a hut. And seriously appreciate that if you are happy and contented with your hut, then you have just jumped over all those people with fancy houses on the seashore, and people like that. You are more rare than them; you have gone far beyond them.

Some people don't get much to eat. Other people, normal people, cook their food and go out to a restaurant once in awhile. Some people get to go to very expensive restaurants and eat fine meals almost every night. And you have leapfrogged over all of them. You get a small simple healthy meal, and you are happy with it. And that's extremely rare. Your karma has gone far beyond the other gourmets.

Some people are not very well informed. They don't read much; they live small lives. Other people read a newspaper fairly frequently and a few books every year. Other people are immersed in information—they are locked in, linked into the web and other places. They know exactly what's going on everywhere. You have leap-frogged over all of them. You have one or two holy, holiest written things in this planet, and you live with them quietly. You should know how far you've come. You are extremely rare on this planet.

Some people have trouble speaking to others. Most people talk most of the day. Some people have great eloquence—they can speak to huge numbers of people. You have jumped over all of them. You have reached silence. That's more rare. The karma to be silent voluntarily is infinitely more rare than eloquence.

Some people don't have many friends; some people have three or four friends; some people are surrounded by admirers. You have jumped over all of them karmi-cally. You are surrounded by a few very devout intense people who are trying to do the most meaningful thing there is. You should know how far you have come. You are not a strange person staying in the desert. Your karma has created this place through thousands of lifetimes of holy effort. You are reaching the culmination of all those efforts. Don't look back. Don't think you haven't come very far—you are here.

Today we might go a little late. It's a custom here; once every teaching we go a little late. I like to think it's in honor of the great debating programs at the great monasteries of Tibet. They do Tsenpe damcha *once a session in the winter debates. That's an all-night debate, and we freeze. And we are tired and exhausted, but we get to have a special porridge and some hot buttered tea, and everyone looks for-ward to it.*

That custom was from a monastery in Tibet called Jang. Holy Lama Rato Rinpoche in New York was the head of that monastery. It was known for its great debaters and logic, and every winter the monks would go and debate for a month—pack up a sleeping bag, pack a bag of food. Hundreds of monks would go to debate the great books on reasoning and perceptual ideas, theories that were started thou-sands of years ago.

When Tibet was lost, this custom was crushed, then it was brought back to life among the monks in India. I think the first winter debates had fifty monks. And then a holy beautiful sacred Lama in America, in New Jersey, put all his money in a trust, and he paid for every monk to go. Now the winter debates have about a thousand of the best monks in the world. So we honor them tonight.

So far we spoke about all the beautiful things we can see. We are honored, we are blessed to see this beautiful sky and the stars at night, especially here—you have to see them tonight after the moon sets. And we can see beautiful mountains, and we can touch the warmth of this earth and see the life of the trees and the creatures who live there. The kindness and the special warmth between beings, even animals, small animals even. We can see each other. Really, I don't think people appreciate the kindness that is flowing on this earth between people already.

I was sent to different factories around the world that make diamonds. My boss made me study the economics of each factory: who could do the best work, which was the best financed, and it took a long time. I came back. I went to meet him; I said, "I've noticed something strange about companies all over the world, and your company too, and all the companies I've ever heard of in this country." I showed him the numbers on the papers. I said, "This is something strange. No one makes any money. No one makes a profit. Every company I've looked at is producing things and selling them cheaper than it costs to make them. And the owners of these companies, the great capitalists, they don't make any money. And they work all day and all night. They have heart attacks and they die. They can't come home to see their children and their families. I don't know what's happening; I don't understand it."

And then much later I realized it's people want to be with each other. People want to make something and offer it to others. The owners of great companies and enterprises, no matter what they do, in the depths of their hearts, they just want to reach out to other people. The roads in this world, which are something completely new and unmatched in history, the travel between places by car, independent of anything, the jet airplanes that take you to Sera in twenty-four hours, to the other side of the world, even the internet and the web.

I don't think you appreciate what is happening. The borders between countries are finally falling down and it will never come back. Anyone who wants to give something to another person, which is what everyone wants to do, can do it directly. The middlemen will die. People will order what they like from the person in the little village in Central America who made it. And each of these things is a sign; they are an expression of the great burning desire of every person to touch other people and serve other people. Don't think it's anything else. We are driven to reach out and to communicate and to serve each other. It's our nature; I think we should be proud of it. To see it is a great joy.

But the things we can't see are much more important. We spoke about them yesterday. The most important things we can't see at all. You have really, if you are honest, no idea where you came from; you've stopped thinking about it many years ago. You're not really sure why you're here, who made this world, what you are supposed to be doing here. You follow other people's examples from the past. You act in a society of others in ways which your parents did, but you're not really sure what we're supposed to do here. And to be honest, very few people have ever seen the other side of death. Very, very few, maybe only one or two in this whole world at this moment. The others are not sure what happened to the people they loved who died. They are not sure if they went on somehow, or stopped. They're not sure if they are suffering or happy now.

And so really almost everyone on this earth is locked into a tiny box. It is exactly one second long. It is about six feet wide. You spend your whole lives locked in a tiny box. Most of your attention is focused, throughout your entire life, on an area about six feet square around you—a little bit bigger than yourself. And you can't see anything beyond these curtains.

I like to think of the space we live in as surrounded by four curtains. There's a curtain in front; there's a curtain to each side, and a curtain behind. Sometimes I stare at what I can see in front of me, and I imagine it's painted on a curtain, and it's just out of my reach. And you live like that. We live in a small box. We are surrounded by four curtains as if we were living in a phone booth or closet. I imagine the edge of what I can see to be just beyond my reach, and then on the back of it is some kind of silver color like a waterfall. And then I imagine all of the time there is stretching out beyond that curtain. So there's a curtain in front, and infinite time and events which will affect me and others, because we will be in them, stretch on forever.

Some silly people say, "No when I die, I'll just stop." There are lots of arguments about why that's silly. I'll give you one.

In a large corporation, you have an MIS department. You have a huge computer, you have terminals stretched out, sometimes through many buildings. Usually the MIS guys stay up all night and run the batch jobs for the next morning. Then sometimes there's a glitch—the machine makes a mistake, and if you're good at MIS, if you run a good computer department, then you just shut it down right away, and you face the heat from the vice presidents who don't have reports the next morning.

Why? Because if you're good at MIS, you know if a machine can make an error once, given the same set of instructions, it will do it again and again. It's inevitable. If a computer which works on pure logic can logically take itself to a breakdown, then you have to find the path it took and stop it, because it will always repeat itself. If you are traveling to Diamond Mountain on a hot day, and you have a car, and it broke down the day before, if you had trouble starting it again, you'd be a fool to make the drive. You have to find out what happened. Any time a car stalls once, the same conditions can make it stall again, and you might be ten miles from any water.

So given infinite time, given that events have an infinite time to repeat a certain series of instructions, it's just foolish to say we can't happen again. It doesn't make any sense at all. Time is infinite; the odds are infinite. Whatever series of events made you happen once will certainly make you happen again, infinitely. That's a little argument; I think it's an undefeatable argument that you do have a future. You will live on somehow.

What I would like to talk about today is how to see it directly. I don't mean with some kind of logic, I mean to see the events of the future as if they were happening two feet from your nose.

Behind us there's a curtain of the past, and I like to think on the left side I imagine holy beings. We have reports of them. Very few people will say directly that they have met them and spoken to them or lived with them. Those beings have a special essence. Their way of being is special. The reason they are divine is that their very essence is a different kind of reality, a higher reality. It's called emptiness in Buddhism, and we'll talk about it later.

Then I always like to think on my right side, behind the curtain, just beyond what I can see, try to imagine countless worlds, planets strung out in lines, and each planet covered with beautiful sparks of life. Beautiful beings, some like you and me and some not, but each different person special, each different person striving to be happy, and going on infinitely, countless worlds. You can learn to see them. I'd like to tell you about a special practice. Then I'd like you, if you'd like, if you want to, then try to practice it in the next few weeks or months. This special practice is called *chulam gyi nelnjor*. *Chulam* means something you do from hour to hour during the day. It means it's not a practice that you do only during your meditation or prayer time. It's a practice you do all day long. *Nelnjor* means yoga. In this case, yoga means a special spiritual practice.

There's a secret version of *chulam gyi nelnjor*, and I can't talk about it to a group. But there's an open practice of *chulam gyi nelnjor*, and I would like you to try it. The way you do it is that every time you remember during the day—it could be every five minutes, it could be every half hour—if you have a busy day or a bad day, it might be six hours. But try, every fifteen or twenty minutes.

Then just for a minute, in the middle of your daily work, whether you are working in an office or whether you are driving somewhere, or whether you are sitting at home, or even if you have already lain down to go to sleep, then you do *chulam gyi nelnjor*.

You imagine a curtain to your right. The front is painted with what you can see, the back is silver like the color of a waterfall or light. And then you just put your hand out. I think try now. Close your eyes and then put your hand out to the right side of you with the palm up. Then you imagine somebody touching your hand almost. You imagine that your hand is reaching through the curtain, like through a waterfall, and you imagine that there's another hand hovering just over your hand. Just a tiny space between them, almost touching, like Michelangelo's hand of Adam and God.

And then you imagine that the person who has that hand is someone you know and love who is in trouble, someone who is ill or someone who is very unhappy, maybe already dead person, someone you used to know and love. You imagine their hand is almost touching you, and they are in grief, they need someone. And you imagine that they can sense that you are reaching for them, and you imagine that they hear you. You say, "I will come; I will help you. I will be the person to come and help you."

21

From what? From their trouble, from hunger and from death itself. "I will come and help you."

And then imagine that the other hand of that person is holding another person's hand, and then another person, and another person. And try to see beyond the curtain that there are worlds upon worlds stretching out infinitely. And I always think of the beings as sitting cross-legged like me, and they are holding hands, and the chain is an infinite chain of people. Between every few thousand people is another planet.

There will come a time, if you learn what I will teach this weekend, that you will see them directly. You will have an experience of them directly. You will be able in a single moment to see every living holy beautiful precious spark of life that exists in all of space, all of this universe. If you do a good *chulam gyi nelnjor,* you plant the seeds for that. You begin the process of drawing that vision to you. So it's very important and it's a joy. It's fun to do *chulam gyi nelnjor.* What could it hurt to imagine that you are comforting every living creature? So pretend, and later it will help it come true.

You can open your eyes now.

If you are working in a busy office and you already have enough problems with the boss thinking you're strange, then you can do holy Lama Khen Rinpoche baseball *chulam nelnjor.* Holy Lama used to bring me upstairs after work. I was exhausted, I was cranky, I was hungry, and he would make me watch baseball. It's very soothing; nothing happens on his TV. And he loved the signs. People stand in the dugout, and they communicate to the players by secret signs. Very tantric. So the coach would stand up, if the batter was really a dangerous one, and he would stare at the pitcher. The pitcher better glance at the dugout every pitch, and he would pull his right ear three times. That's a neutral sign. That means, "I'm trying to give you a sign."

Then he would touch his chest and spit tobacco, and those are false signs for the opposition. Then they think that every time someone spits tobacco, someone is going to hit a home run, or something. Then he gives the real sign—the fifth sign is always the real sign—like he might touch his nose. And your *chulam gyi nelnjor* should be like that. Secret practices are much more powerful than the ones that you tell everybody. When you do something only because it's important to do, when you do something that no one will ever know that you did it to help someone, it's much more powerful. I read that in "Dear Abby." If you do things for others secretly, then it's very powerful. She said. And other great texts say that.

So make a few secret signs for your *chulam gyi nelnjor.* Like you could just pretend that you are snapping your fingernail, like you're nervous maybe. Or you could just scratch behind your ear. Or anything like that. And it's a statement to yourself and to all those suffering holy creatures on the other side of the curtain. It's a sign. You have to explain the signs in the locker room. When you go home tonight and you're by yourself, when you sit in front of an image of a holy being like Lord Buddha or Khen Rinpoche, and you say, "I'm going to make a deal with you. Every time I touch my ear like that, it means, 'I'm trying to help you. I'm trying to come to help all those precious holy creatures who live.'"

It's important to say it out loud at least once. And you just make a promise like that, "When I remember, which may not be very often if I'm very busy or distracted, but if you see me touch my ear like that, you beings, then you should know that I'm thinking of you. I want to see you all. I want to see all the pain you have, and I swear I will help you."

And you can do this yoga anywhere, any time. It's a very holy practice. It plants extremely powerful seeds in your mind. It's the very first step to seeing those beings directly and being able to serve them, which is all we all really want to do—we just forgot a little.

So try tonight, the first *nelnjor.* There will be four yogas, one for each curtain. Practice tonight. We'll practice during this talk. You have to get used to this subtle interruption of your day for a few seconds, and then going back to your work or your life.

I'd like it if you could have some refreshments now and relax and enjoy each other's company, as we enjoy. We can feel you when you're here. We can't sleep much *[laughs].* Everyone looked very tired before they put on the blindfolds, but it's a sweet feeling of not sleeping. It's feeling your happiness and the warmth of having you here. So please have some refreshment.

Now we'll start the actual instructions for how to see behind those four curtains. Today we will only cover five stages that your mind goes through as you attempt to draw those objects closer to you. I like to think of it like a big fishing pole, and you hook them and you draw them closer and closer through five stages, and then finally the curtains drop. And I would like to repeat that you will never be able to do this until you do it for others. And very simply, everyone around us is dying. It is as if we are halfway down the mouth of some horrible creature already.

So you have to remember that when you try to bring the four curtains down. Deep in your heart you have to want to help the people who are struggling in this life, facing an inevitable painful death and the destruction of everything they ever tried to do. If you have this feeling, if you try to remember it from hour to hour, like when you do your *chulam gyi nelnjor*, your hour-to-hour yoga, then you will be able. And if you don't, you will never be able. Then tomorrow we will talk about the actual practices you have to do to train yourself to see beyond the four curtains. And then on Sunday we'll talk about why those practices really work, and I think if you hear how they really work, then you will have confidence and you will try.

The first of the five stages of your mind is called *Viparyaya*. This teaching comes from the ancient books on *pramana*, the ancient books on how to think clearly, how to perceive things that are difficult to perceive. The main book was written around 600 AD by Master Dharmakirti. He was writing an explanation of his master's work, Dignaga.

In Tibet, the greatest explanations were written by three disciples of Je Tsongkapa. Je Tsongkapa was the founder of our lineage. He lived 600 years ago. He was the teacher of the first Dalai Lama, and oftentimes in his wisdom, he would ask his students to write the books so that the lineage would be passed on. And so Gendun Drup, the first Dalai Lama, His Holiness, wrote a good solid textbook on how to perceive these deep things. Then Kedrup Je, who is sometimes called Je Tsongkapa's tantric master disciple, the one who specialized in the tantric lineages, he wrote an amazing commentary called *Tsema Dedun Yi Kyi Munsel*, and it's a commentary on the seven great books of *pramana,* or reasoning, from ancient India. This is a very good textbook for westerners; it's laid out like a western textbook.

But the greatest work of all was by Gyaltsab Je, Darma Rinchen. It's called *Namdrel Tarlam Selje,* "A Light for the Path to Freedom." Gyaltsab Je was Je Tsongkapa's greatest disciple. He absorbed thousands of pages of learning from his master. After the master's passing, he was granted the throne of the master. Someone asked him, "What was the kindest thing Je Tsongkapa ever did to you? Was it a

24

tantric teaching? Was it meditational instructions? Was it a vision of a deity?" He said, "No, he taught me reasoning. He taught me how to see things that you can't see." And then he wrote the greatest book.

In the winter debates, the monks from the greatest monasteries, the cream of the monasteries, come to one of the monasteries. They meet for a month; they debate non-stop. They take rest at night for a whole month. You might debate for a week on a page of Gyaltsab Je's 400-page commentary.

The greatest modern master of this learning, the holder of this lineage, was Geshe Yeshe Wangchuk, who passed away a few years ago. His greatest disciple is Geshe Thubten Rinchen, who many of you had the honor of learning with in Sera Monastery. And these lineages go back to Lord Buddha, and to even older times and other planets.

I would like to teach you from one of those books. Before you came to this talk, how were you thinking about the possibility of seeing exactly, precisely, directly what you will be after you die? I think many of us maybe, I don't know who you are, but many of us weren't thinking about it at all. We didn't think it was possible to see that thing. And so our mind was in a kind of darkness.

This is the first of the five stages. I like to picture it like a journey from a dark land, like an evil island that never sees the sunlight. It is the land of, "Oh that can't be, I can't see that, no one has seen that." We have reports of people who have seen special things, but it's difficult to confirm. It's not common nowadays to meet people who have seen beyond those four curtains. And so most of us are living on this dark island called *Viparyaya*.

The root text says, *Viparyayo mithyajnanam atadrupa pratishtam*. *Viparyaya* in Tibetan is *loktok*. *Loktok* means completely wrong idea, completely opposite wrong ass-backwards. *Viparyaya* says, "I can't see that thing. People don't see their future. I can hardly believe that someone sitting in front of me might be at this minute seeing what will happen to them in five hundred years."

And *mithyajnanam* means wrong, very wrong thinking, very wrong idea. *Atadrupa pratishtam*. It is mired, it is stuck in complete misconception. It's like a dark island.

25

At this point in the first stage, the object, what's going to come to you, and all the places where beings live and all the sweet holy sparks of life, human, animal, and other, these are at this stage, complete darkness. You don't even have a clue. So you have to leave this island behind, and go. I like to think of the next step as the ocean.

Now if this was a business meeting at work or if this was a conversation over lunch with some friends, or if this was a TV show that you were watching in your armchair, it's time to do *chulam gyi nelnjor.* It's time to make your secret sign to third base coach. So try; practice now. This is how *chulam nelnjor* works. You just interrupt your regular program and for a few seconds, you close your eyes, you put your hand out to the right. You make your own secret sign tonight when you announce it in the locker room. You imagine that some sweet person that you love is trying to touch your hand through the curtain, and is just a tiny fraction of an inch away from touching you.

One day you will really feel it. And then in a long, infinitely long human chain, we are pretending, visualizing all the other creatures as humans, then stretches from planet to planet. And you comfort them, and you say, "I am learning. I am really trying hard. I will come and help you. I will be able."

Then you take your hand back and you open your eyes. When you get good at it, it takes only a few seconds. Your boss wonders why you scratch your ear all the time. Make it on the right side; we have to save the other sides.

The second stage that the mind goes through, I like to think of it as like an ocean, like you've left that dark island. You're headed toward a safe country, but first you have to go across the ocean. This ocean is called *Vikalpa.* In the root text, it says, *Shabdajnana anupati vastushunyah vikalpah. Shabdajnana anupati* means at this point you only have a very rough picture in your mind, an image of what *might* be possible. *Vikalpa* is like an ocean of the might be. Maybe I could do it. The guy seems pretty convinced I could do it. Maybe.

This is still not *pramana* yet. *Pramana* means true vision, true perception. Why? *Vastushunyo.* The rough idea you have in your mind is so rough that we can't say it's almost anything like the real thing that you're going to reach when the curtains come down. But it's a start, isn't it? It's a rough idea. You've got these ten or twelve balls in your mind that are supposed to be planets, and there's a bunch of squiggly lines called people and they're holding hands, and you're starting to get a rough picture. In the study of perception, there are different states within *vikalpa*. One is called *yichu* in Tibetan. It means like a rough guess or a rough estimate, like, "If I had to make sort of a half-educated guess, I would say he's talking about something like this." And then a little picture pops into your mind.

There's another kind of *vikalpa* called *dungyur gyi tetsom* in Tibetan, and it means some shyness or kind of doubt. Here the word doubt means a suspicion: "Maybe, maybe that's true. Maybe I could do what he's talking about." *Dungyur kyi tetsom* means the "maybe" is getting hot; the "maybe" is getting warm. You're headed the right way. You're headed away from the maybe that says, "Maybe not." You're headed towards the maybe that says, "Maybe could." And that's called *vikalpa*.

I think of it as a mist over the ocean. You are making pictures that aren't very clear. You've been listening to me yesterday and today; you're starting to percolate this idea that you could see every single living creature and all the worlds they live in in one moment. Or you could meet directly beings who have evolved into the perfection of ultimate reality and have actually become that, who had the power to show themselves on infinite planets at once. You're starting to think, "He wouldn't waste so much time talking about something that's totally crazy. Maybe, maybe there's something there." Then when you start to think like that, you've reached the second stage called *vikalpa*.

Shabdajnana anupati means the mind follows a picture based on words. We distinguish *drachi* from *dunchi*. *Drachi* means a picture in your mind of something that you've never seen before. Khen Rinpoche, holiest lama in the universe, used to say "Eiffel Tower." He had never seen the Eiffel Tower, but he had heard about it, so he had a *drachi*, he had an image based on someone's description. A *dunchi* is an image that you have of something you've really seen, like the Dragoon Mountain in front of you, and then if you go home, and someone says, "What's that mountain?" an image comes into your mind. That's a *dunchi*.

When you have *vikalpa*, the second stage, you are only as far as a picture that comes from someone's description, and that's called *shabdajnana anupati*.

Let's do *chulam nelnjor*. Close your eyes, reach out to your right, imagine your hand is on the other side of the silver curtain. Someone you know, maybe someone you loved who passed away, is there, expectantly waiting for you. They know

27

you're alive; they know you are getting close to having the power to really help. And their finger is only a tiny fraction of an inch from yours, and you imagine touching their hand, and comforting them, and saying, "I'll come, I'm learning, I'll help you and all the people whose hands you hold." Then you snap back into your lunchtime conversation. This is real *chulam gyi nelnjor.* Even the secret one is the same pattern, for those of you who are trying.

The third stage I like to think of as a beautiful big beach, and then a long, I imagine yellow, plain, a flat plain like Kansas, and covered with some kind of golden wheat or something. It's a long plain, flat land, and you jump from the ship. You touch ground. You leap from the ocean on to the solid land. There's a reason for this metaphor. This is the first time you've gone from "maybe" to "it is." You've gone from not *pramana* to *pramana. Pramana* means true perception, valid perception—you're right, 100 percent right.

There are three kinds of *pramana.* In the text, it says, *pratyaksha anymana agamah pramanani.* It means there are three kinds. First you get *agama.* I like to think of *agama* as this solid land, because for the first time you've passed from thinking some dim idea about helping all living creatures to a very firm knowledge: "I can do it!" This is the greatest leap you have to make. I don't think anyone here would have a lot of trouble imagining helping every living creature, but to really make the leap from thinking it's only maybe possible to being absolutely certain that is possible, is where most of us stop. We never touch the dry land; we're stuck on the ocean. You have to try very hard to make this leap; it is the most difficult passage.

What is *agama? Agama* in Tibetan is called *lung. Agama pramana* is called *lung gi tsema.* It means you have confronted, you have made contact with a person who can see through the four curtains already. And you spend time with them, and you talk with them, and then finally you come to a realization that what they are describing is true. The scriptures are extremely strict about this kind of perception because it requires that you establish that the person speaking is telling the absolute truth. And it's very difficult to establish within the strict rules—we call the command of logic—that the person speaking to you must be telling the truth, must be describing something which has really happened.

How do you establish that a person is telling the truth about something neither you nor almost anyone has ever seen? It comes from establishing that the person speaking, and I am also referring to books and scriptures, accounts from people

28

who are not here anymore. *Agama* comes from establishing that this person must be speaking the truth. Why? Because they speak the truth about other things. If you think about it, this is a very delicate line. You are staking your life's pursuits on the belief that a person who speaks the truth about some things must also be speaking the truth about amazing beautiful things beyond those curtains.

How can we establish that this person is speaking truly, maybe even from experience? The test in scripture is very interesting. Do they speak of the most important things of all? And in spiritual things, it means does this person speak about suffering? Throughout our lives, people either sugarcoat our condition or outright lie to us. When my dear holy father was very ill, I remember the people took us into a room. They said, "Be cheerful. No one say what really is going on. No use to trouble a person who is going to die shortly."

And so in our culture, whether you admit it or not, we are encouraged not to look at what is really happening. Every person here is in the grips of the lord of death. Every person around you is halfway down the powerful jaws and fangs of a horrible invisible thing called the lord of death. Like the child rabbit, we scratch at the ground, trying to pull ourselves away, and the leg is already being torn apart. What are the chances that you can get someone out of this if you can't even do it for yourself? So we don't talk about it. But if you ever come across a person who speaks openly, frankly, truly, and then it strikes a chord in your heart, "Oh this is really the most important thing of all; how can we stop this suffering that every human creature and every other living thing has to go through?" If a person will stand up and stake their life, their life's work, their life's time, their life's money on trying to stop this suffering, then, the scriptures say, listen to them when they speak about the way. That's the basis for *agama*.

Agama means the speech of a person who cannot be lying. And if you ever meet such a person, then you can take what they say as truth with no other proof than that. This is the hardest leap to make, perhaps because it's so hard to find a source of *agama*. It is the first great leap all of us would have to make. But if you meet that person, and they describe the method clearly and if you are convinced that they must be speaking truth, especially the truth from personal experience, then what you see is real. You have gone from unreal to real. It's not a vague image anymore, however rough and unclear it is.

You are seeing the truth. The image that you have in your mind, if you have established that this person who is speaking cannot be lying, is a true one. You are really seeing the possibility, the inevitability of being able to see what will come to you after you die. You are beginning to see the inevitable vision of being able to see every single place there is in a single moment and every being who lives in those places, the ones you are going to save, and at the same time, you have a true image of the existence of holy enlightened beings around us constantly, who are struggling to bring us to our full destiny. The image is true. You have crossed onto the dry land of *agama*.

I'd like to take another break there. We thought it might get cold, but I don't think so. *[Laughs.]* But pull out some drinks and snacks and bring them to your place. We'll pretend we're at the winter debates. We just sit there and ignore the debates and concentrate on the porridge and the tea. So please have some refreshments and then we'll continue.

Now we've followed the state of mind through three stages. The first was the dark island. "I think it's impossible to see directly what I will become in the very end of things." Then you go to the second stage, which is, "Oh, maybe I could see that." Then the third stage is, "I will see that," because a person described it who cannot be lying. That's a hard leap to make, the last one, and you shouldn't try to make it until you are sure. It won't be made until you are sure that the person speaking is telling the absolute truth.

These are the three states of mind so far. In the monastery, in a debate, we would be tracking the condition of the object as well. What you will become in the end of all ends is for the first state of mind, only darkness. What you will become at the very end of all things, is for the second state of mind, only a dim picture. What each of us will inevitably become, for the third state of mind is a very sharp picture, and the object has crossed into the state of reality. It is a true image of something. It corresponds to an actual object. It isn't *vastushunya* anymore. It's not something which no longer corresponds to an object. It now represents something that really exists. We call the object at this stage in the fishing process—drawing in the object to your mind, bringing it through the curtain—we call that object *shintu kokgyur. Shintu kokgyur* means real, but very difficult to see.

Then the object comes closer and closer; it becomes just *chungse kokgyur. Chungse kokgyur* means difficult but not so difficult to see anymore. That's at the fourth stage. The fourth stage is called *anumana pramana. Pramana* means true perception, *anumana* means, in Tibetan, *jepak. Jepak tsema* is when you sit down and

30

think it out clearly, and after many hours of thinking hard about it, you can establish that you could see beyond the curtain to the future directly. You work it out in your mind, slowly, carefully. You think about all the arguments that were given in favor of this idea, and then suddenly one day, it just clicks, and you perceive what you will become with a new clarity, with a greater clarity. It's no longer very far away and hidden to your eyes; it's much closer. The image is sharper. The process of reasoning has now demanded and created a stronger image.

On Sunday, I would like to have the honor, really, of speaking about the emptiness of this image, but I feel like it's useful to give you a small introduction now so that the seeds are planted. Also I don't think you get the real feeling of the winter debates if you don't suffer a little tonight. Some people listening to the talk this evening will be polite, but honestly they won't think it very meaningful or immediately applicable to their life. They are interested. They wouldn't come to this lonely isolated place in the desert and take the trouble that you have all taken, and the expense to come here lightly, but after a few days, they will dismiss it because they didn't really grasp it. Maybe a few fortunate people we call *kelwa sangpo*, people who have been extraordinarily kind to others in the past, and so their minds are free and open—they will be stunned. *Kelwa sangpo* people start crying at strange times; they get bristles of hairs rising up their spine when they hear about these holy things, even if they have never heard about them before.

And so these words that I'm saying even now are empty. Empty means they don't have any quality of their own. If the words I'm saying were from their own side convincing and important to everyone, then everyone would be struck, and everyone tonight would do their *nelnjor* locker room secret code ritual, and immediately they would start on the journey to tear down the four curtains. If the words I'm speaking tonight from their own side were sort of a little mixed-up, crazy and the words of a person who spent too long in a little hut, then everyone would go home and try to get a meal before the two restaurants in 100 miles close.

But my words are empty, so if you are experiencing them as meaningful, it must be something in your own mind, some sweet holy extraordinary rare seed, *samskara*, which is causing you to hear them in a holy way. And then if you find these words a little interesting but dull, then it must be coming from some part of your mind also. That's what emptiness means—it's no more mysterious than that. You don't have to argue or debate about it. It's obvious. My words aren't meaningful from their own side. Your mind, if you have the great fortune, finds the meaning in them. My words aren't dull or boring from their own side. If you find them dull or boring, it's a part of your mind which is making them dull and boring. My words are empty of any quality of being meaningful or boring. That's the emptiness of my words.

So something very important. When I talk about drawing in an object through the curtain, when I say there's an object out there, there are countless planets, worlds, realms even, around us, and in those worlds and realms are lovely, holy, striving, beautiful creatures, life like us. And then if I ask you, "Is that object existent or not? Does it exist or not? Do there exist these sweet, struggling, striving creatures like us, everywhere, limitless? Does that object exist or not? And then what is the status of it? If it does exist, is it *shintu kokgyur?* Is it very, very far away and very hard to see, or is only *chun se kokgyur*, is it sort of hard to see? Or is it *ngongyur, pratyaksha*, is it right in front of your face?"

Then those of you who have studied emptiness, I'm sure you will reply, "For whom?"

We were at Ganden in the winter debates. Holy Lama Trijang Rinpoche allowed me to stay at his holy residence. I was stuck in the middle of big group of people who wanted to see what a white guy could do. So you always start a debate with a controversial statement. It will at least confuse the other people until you have time to get away. So they said, "Is such-and-such an object *shintu kokgyur*, very difficult to see, or *chungse kokgyur*, kind of difficult to see, or is it *ngongyur*, is it right in front of your face?"

I said, "All goddam three!" You have to have a little *chutzpah* in debate. And thank God, for hours they couldn't figure it out. And only much later I realized I had hit upon something that great books talk about. Of course everything is all three. Every object is all three.

"What are you talking about? What about the sky, the blue sky? That's in front of our faces. That's *pratyaksha*. That's right in front of you."

For whom? Not for a blind man. He can't see the blue. For a blind man, the blue of the sky is not evident, it's not obvious reality. It's a deeper reality.

"The vision of countless planets and holy, sweet, expectant beings on those plan-

32

ets, is it hard to see or not?" You have to say, "For whom?"

So all things are hard to see, and all things are easy to see, because none of them is hard to see from its side. Nothing is hidden from its side. Nothing is open from its side. This is the key to seeing beyond the four curtains. I have given you a clue. Holiest Lama, sweet darling Khen Rinpoche would say, "Now go home and cook it."

The fifth state of mind...*Oh,* chu lam nelnjor. *Close your eyes. Put your right hand out and touch them. Promise to come soon. OK, come back. At work it will be that fast.*

The fifth state of mind is called *pratyaksha. Pratyaksha* means right in front of your eyes. If you hold up your hand in front of your face and look at your palm, that's what we call *pratyaksha pramana.* That's *ngunsum tsema* in Tibetan, direct perception. You see it as if it were in the palm of your hand, they say. The goal of this teaching is to learn how to bring those holy objects under the curtain, through the curtain and make them *pratyaksha.* Establishing that these things are possible by logic is like going from the plain up to the foothills. Then *pratyaksha,* direct perception, is like climbing a beautiful high mountain.

I was thinking of visiting towns like Dharamsala, and when you take the bus down, you look out the window, and the Himalayas fill half the sky. It's a very strange feeling. You feel like maybe they're going to fall down on you and squash you. So I was thinking of *pratyaksha* as looking up at those mountains with their white snow in the bright sun from the Indian plain. That's direct perception—right in front of your face.

There will come a day when you look up. You will see what you are going to become. In the very end, you will see those worlds and those beings. You will see divine beings. They will instruct you. You will see their core, which is ultimate reality. The seeds are being planted now.

There's one more image, and then I'll stop. I thought it would help you to remember the five stages of the mind. I was thinking of one of those holy, sweet, infinitely kind careladies who are sacrificing their own life and time and money, and their own practice so that we can practice. And many others like them, but those three more than anyone.

33

So suppose caretaker Venerable Jigme Palmo, Elly-hla, is sitting in her little house that I've heard about—I've never seen. Her roommate is bouncing around, clicking on the floor with his half chewed-off leg, and she's ordered some vegetables from someone, oh, in Benson. They're not very reliable; they promised to deliver them on Thursday. Then on Wednesday, the day before, she hears some sound, a car. She's trying to figure out if it's some people running drugs down our road from Mexico, or maybe some campers who have started a forest fire, so she decides to go look.

At the moment she's at her door, her mind is in the state of mind number one, *viparyaya*. It hasn't even crossed her mind that maybe the guy who she can't count on is bringing vegetables early, a day early. It's darkness, it's a kind of mental darkness and it's wrong. Then she starts walking towards the kitchen, which I've never heard about, I've never seen, but certainly enjoyed, and outside she sees a car pulling away, driving off, and she thinks maybe she's seen it before. She has some dim image in her mind. "That looks a lot like the car of that undependable vegetable guy."

At this point, the state of mind is *vikalpa*. There's an image forming in her mind of the vegetables. It's a very dim image; it doesn't correspond to a real vegetable yet, you see? She goes to the door of the kitchen yurt. She looks in. Sweet Venerable Chukyi-hla is there. She is leaning over. She's got the refrigerator door open. She's got her head halfway in. Venerable Jigme Palmo, Elly-hla, can't see inside, because it's a side view, but she can see that holy Anne is looking in, and she says, "Are there any vegetables in there? Is there a box of vegetables in there?"

And Venerable holy sweet life-giving Anne turns towards her and nods her head and says, "Yes."

This is *agama*. This is *agama*. Venerable Jigme Palmo knows Venerable Anne, being a nun, wouldn't lie about small things like vegetables. And this is the basis of *agama*. *Agama* means you totally at that moment trust this person about that thing. Why should anyone lie about such a thing? And they have a long history together; they've known each other a long time. This is a good example of *agama*. Anne has never spoken anything but truth, and we know it, and she says vegetables are there, and then in Venerable Jigme Palmo, holy angel hla's mind, this strong, solid image of vegetables comes. This is now *pramana*; this is now a true perception. There's an actual box that corresponds to the solid picture in Venerable Jigme

Palmo's holy lady's mind.

Then she starts to walk towards the refrigerator, and I imagine a table there, and on the table is a big invoice, a bill. It's from "Joe Shmoe Vegetable Company." It says "one box of vegetables, such-and-such price," and in big letters it says, "and I delivered it a day early!"

Then Venerable Jigme Palmo, holy being, precious one, says in her mind, "He must have come." And the box of vegetables, the image, the true image, *vero nika*, gets stronger. And you know the end of the story. She walks up next to holy Anne —Amber's out working somewhere—and she looks in the refrigerator, and there's a big box of vegetables. And that's *pratyaksha*, that's direct perception.

So what we hope to do is go through the same process. We hope to tear down the curtain in front and see directly what will become of us. We hope to tear down the curtain to our right, and in a single moment, see every world there is and every living creature waiting for us to help them. Imagine what will happen on that day. Your life will be changed forever. You can't say anymore, "I can't do it," or "I don't know about it."

Imagine how your life will change on that day. You will change entirely inside. This is the real feeling of *bodhichitta*. You will never be able to spend another hour of your life without working to serve them, and help them and save them. We will tear down the curtain behind, which is where we came from, and we will tear down the curtain to the left, which is all the holy beings who are guiding us without us even knowing it, and their true nature, which is the key to everything, their emptiness.

These seeds are being planted as we speak. If you haven't seen these things, then you will, it will come. Remember to do it for others, or it will never come. These things are always completely hidden to people who can't do it for others.

Have a good night and we will miss you, and try to remember to prepare your secret sign and then start doing it. And we are really very grateful. I don't think any of us in retreat will ever be able to repay you. It's a very heavy feeling, very grave responsibility, but you should know that each of these people has really tried hard to the limit, and sometimes even a little too far, to earn the hard work you are doing for us. So we all thank you all the time. Good night.

Third Day:

Saturday, September 22, 2001

III.

Leave the dark world
On the ship of openness,
Hope, and innocence.

Cross to the highlands
On the steed of learning;
Use the staff of contemplation
To come to the base of the peaks.

The mountains can only be scaled
With the rope of meditation;
The sun of the Beings of Light
Shines upon them all.

Tu sam gom sum:
The ways of wisdom are old
And have not aged a day.

First find a Guide who knows the way
Both by head and foot;
The hour to hour, and a friend.

Then take yourself to the classics;
A voice in a thousand years.
Commit the directions to memory

The song within your head,
A companion for you and others
Whenever you need; select.

Walk; take small and steady steps
Circle thrice, then once for meaning
At the end half again, for firmness.

Sing along beads, watch for holes,
Return at times, use your time.
Be graceful when it flies;
Nothing is lost, and never too late.

Swim in the pool,
Cherish the flower;
Four sips of nectar,
Kept in a crystal jar.
Mull it over in silence,
Then turn the talk to meaning.

Crush the demons
Of sloth and pride and envy.
Go to the dark room first,
Together; question, feel the joy
Of discovery unfolding.

Dance and clap,
But don't forget your gun;
Bring Jampa with
To carry it.

Once the target is clear,
Sit.
Silent place,
Silent body,
Silent mind.

Master the process—

Preliminaries, antidotes;
And then improve it;
Inch the bar up on Monday,
Circle back for victory.

Reach the seventh direct,
Tear down the curtains.
Follow threads of the Dharma
To go behind:
Reach up and touch your shoulder.

I thought first to meditate for a few minutes.

Holy Lama Khen Rinpoche, Great Lama, used to call me up to his room to watch a TV show. And I think he liked the advertisements better than the shows. There was one awhile back. There was a gruff old man who acted as a college professor in a TV show, and he was making an advertisement for an investment company. And he said, "We make money the old way. We earn it!" Rinpoche really loved that.

It reminds me of the retreatants. They have been here, I think this week or next week it's a year and a half; it's half way. And they've earned what they've reached. The first year was a lot like freshman year in college. Everything goes wrong, and you're lonely for your family and your old friends, and you're confused. You don't know where the classes are held and the teachers all seem mean, and the other students are all smarter.

It's hard the first year; I think even the body needs time to adjust to such an extreme place. Our houses weren't really finished when we came. Lots of strange creatures would crawl in and we didn't know how to close them up. It got really, really cold. And then obviously it's very hot also.

But this is an old idea in ancient times, up to modern times. It's called, in Sanskrit, tapas. Tapas is a beautiful word. It means to burn something hard. Like if you have a clay pot and you put it in an oven and fire it for a whole day– that's like tapas. And then the pot comes out hard. Or if you take a sword, like the great

Irish Diamond Mountain sword, and you put it in a hot fire and the fire makes it shine and blaze with red-hot heat, and then afterwards it comes out hardened and tempered. I think even the word "temper" comes from the same word as tapas. So tapas means to burn yourself a little, and afterwards you come out harder. In Tibetan the translated word was katup. Ka means "hard to do." Tup means "I can do it." And I think that each of the retreatants has shown in the best way, by their actions, that they got hard and tough.

There's talk about making the places a little more comfortable. Maybe putting in some real water. Maybe, you know, improvements. I say, "No." I think it's good for people, and people throughout history have used tapas. I think that the people who come here for deep retreat—I'm not talking about short-term visitors—but the people who come for serious retreat should be serious. And they should be tested and fired. I don't think you can sit with your mind all day and fight with it if you can't face a rattlesnake.

And so the blessing of tapas has come to each of the retreatants. One is very allergic to bees. One bee sting would create a mark on her arm for several years. So of course she's the only one who's been bitten by three or four. She spent three days in a delirium, alone, in her bed. This is tapas. Another retreatant was bitten by a rattlesnake. She was in the hospital. She came back. She just sat down and started to meditate. We saw her several weeks later and her eyes were still wandering around.

Another retreatant lived in the city her whole life. She was nervous about the countryside, being alone in the dark much of the time. So of course a big rattlesnake moved under her yurt the first week. He wouldn't leave. Everyone tried. He would rattle every time she walked to remind her. But she toughed it out. A special man came and took the snake away.

Another retreatant sits on her porch at night watching the stars. It's the only ten or fifteen minute break of the day. And a huge form smashes through the gate, a wolf or coyote has decided he likes to see her. And then he would come back, I think for weeks.

So everyone has been tested. I think I can say every single one of us has had very serious emotional difficulties. We've invented a word for it. It's called "mind crash." And you just get sad and cry for a day, or you act crazy for a day, or you get angry for a day, or you just feel lost for a day.

But now that freshman year is over, I think we feel like sophomores. Sophomores know everything. And each of the retreatants has gotten really tough and hard. And there are beautiful things coming out of the tapas. One retreatant has done a beautiful, huge, moment-by-moment description of all of the visualizations in our sadhana. It's a very long sadhana—our daily prayers, meditations—and she's done a beautiful sequence script for each meditation, each detail.

Another retreatant has done beautiful illustrations of many of the special breathing practices that we do, and she's also done a beautiful book on the ancient practice of tormas, which are special offering, how to make special offering cakes in the secret tradition. Another retreatant undertook to make a manual of all the problems that people might face in the future, trying to do what we are trying to do. And then each retreatant contributed the things they have found to help. That retreatant also is undergoing very difficult special practices called sindhur langali. And we'll be doing some special practices more.

Another retreatant has been drawn to do a study of the ancient Sanskrit books which the practices we are learning have come from, and has done very well. Another retreatant has written up a beautiful course of study, like questions and answers about the entire practices of our sadhana. And these are all just spontaneous. They just are coming out from the tapas.

So I think we should keep this place tough. It acts as a filter. People who can't take it won't stay. And the ones who stay will be serious. I think someone expressed concern about the lack of any water at all under this earth. And I think it's great. I think real meditators should live in a tiny place. They should work hard. They should live off a gallon of water a day for all their needs.

In Sera monastery in Tibet, Holy Lama told me they were not allowed to have any covering on the windows. They were supposed to be, learn tapas in the cold. In the debate ground they would debate: usually every other day is two sessions, six hours, and then every other day is one session, three hours, and then one day off. It was so cold that they would bury themselves in the ground up to their waist to stay warm. No monk was allowed to wear a cloak until you reached senkyang dangpo. This is, oh, fifteen years.

I don't think you know, and I don't think Khen Rinpoche, holy Lama, has told many people, after the first twelve years of study it's a custom to go in retreat to prepare for the holy study of Madhyamika, emptiness, Middle Way.

Khen Rinpoche, holy [cries], went to a cave above Sera in the mountains. He got very ill. He was alone. He almost passed. Even in India, in modern times, the monks at Sera and the other holy great monasteries, sit in the sun for hour after hour. The debate ground used to be a big, muddy field. You came home covered with dirt. Your voice was gone. Your face was burnt. Your hands are split open and bleeding. It used to be a problem. You would say, "Could you slap your hands to the side. The blood spurts in my eyes." And there was no water at Sera. There was a small stream of mud about two hundred yards down the hill. People tried to drink it. I couldn't even drink it. This is tapas.

Holy Lama Geshe Thubten Rinchen lived for twenty years in a hut with clay tiles broken on the top. The students would sit in class and get soaked. Geshe-hla would shift around his bed, which was his teaching throne, and try to avoid the water coming down.

Holy Lama Yeshe Tomden, great debater from Sera, would live in a stone hut in the mountains above Dharamsala, His Holiness' place. He would travel to countries in the West. He would be offered thousands of dollars. I saw him come to Sera. He was distinctive because he refused to change his robes, which had ripped off and covered only down to his knees. But he wouldn't spend a few dollars on himself. He humbly offered all the money to feed the monks at Sera. And he would [cries], back to his stone hut and he died there. I think it's an honor to follow their example.

If you have a group of people practicing tapas, and you have an equally dedicated group of people helping them, amazing things come out. We have everything we need. We ask for a book, it just appears quickly. We need to know something for our practice. The caretakers go and look it up in the database of thousands of holy books, still being input furiously due to efforts of kind people sitting here. Holy wisdom being saved for the future. Any time we need special food, medicines, they just come immediately. Any time we have a problem it's solved immediately. We have holy, beautiful masters of different skills who come and teach us. We are so lucky. We have the best.

41

And so it's like we are the tapas and you are the fuel, and it's a beautiful thing. I think we should try to keep this tradition of being hard-asses here. It doesn't mean that we shouldn't make comfortable places for people who are not well, or who can't physically do difficult things. It doesn't mean that we shouldn't have classes in comfortable places for new people, or people who aren't used to difficulty. But the real serious ones should be joyful to carry on this tradition of tapas. We aren't allowed by our vows to hurt our body. Our body is a very holy, precious temple. We have to take very good care of it. But within those rules we should be tough.

We've been talking about how to see things that almost no one can see. Where do we really come from? What are we supposed to do while we're here? What will happen to us later?

We spoke about five stages that the mind goes through. First you don't believe you could see those three things. Then later you start to think maybe you could. After that, you get some training and you start to believe it is possible. Then you work on it and the vision gets deeper and stronger, and then finally it opens into reality, direct perception. You can see exactly what you will evolve into in the final moments of limitless time you have lived. You know how long it will take to get there, and it's an unbelievable feeling. You could help so many people if you could impart to them the instructions for doing this. People would be free from every fear.

If you work hard, you can reach a point where you see every single place where beings live in this world and in countless other worlds. You can see every living being who lives on those worlds, and you can know that you'll be able to serve them and help them. All in a moment's time. Your mind is freed from the limits, from the little box we stay in. Space has no meaning any more. You can see all things, all places. Even before enlightenment. And you can see the holy beings who exist around us. You can meet, talk to them. You can receive help from them. And, most importantly, you can learn to see their core, the very inner essence of them, which is a higher truth. And that truth actually underlies all existence that we are aware of. All these things which we can't see, you can learn to see.

Today I would like to talk about the old way of seeing these things. I would like to talk about the traditional methods. They are thousands of years old and they haven't aged a day. You have to try to respect and learn them, because they work. To go from *viparyaya*, the black island, which is "I don't believe I could see every living creature at once," and to cross into the ocean of *vikalpa*, which is "Maybe I could do it," you need innocence. You have to be like a child again.

We get more and more hard and jaded and calcified as we get older. We don't have dreams or visions or faith that special things are possible. So you need a kind of innocence. You have to be open to special ideas. You can't say, "Oh, I never heard of anyone seeing all the people who live, all the creatures who live."

Be like a child. Be open to the idea. Hope. You haven't lived that long. Time is endless. You haven't seen anything. Every time I said to holy Lama Khen Rinpoche, "Wow, I never heard of that," he would scowl. He'd say, "There's lots of things you haven't heard of."

Then to cross the long plain of *agama* and reach the foothills, you need a strong horse. *Agama* means a belief that these holy things are possible and that you could do it, because someone you totally believe in has sworn these things are possible. Perhaps they've even seen them themselves.

That horse is the learning we call *tu*. In Sanskrit, *shruti*. It means "listening." Then in the foothills, to reach the high mountains, in the foothills of *anumana*, you need a strong walking stick—agaves are great, they're light and strong, the sticks that grow here on the plants. That walking stick is called *chinta*. It means "contemplation." You think about what you've heard. In Tibetan, *sampa*.

And then to get to the height of the mountain, the mountains are *pratyaksha*, direct perception. Of what? Of what you'll be. Direct. See it directly. Of countless beings. See them all and know you will help them. You will be the one. Direct contact with what you would call angels. Having them teach you.

To see their essence you need a rope to climb that mountain. The rope is meditation. So in Tibetan, and in our lineage for thousands of years: *tu sam gom sum, tu sam gom sum*. Listen, think about what you've heard, and then meditate on it. This is how you can see the things that you didn't even believe you could see. I would like to talk about each of those steps today, and then tomorrow I'll explain why they work.

Because we are blessed, we live in a very skeptical country. Buddha loved skeptical people because once you've shown them good reasons, they will understand

and they will move. Then people who just believe everything you say skip from thing to thing and end up with nothing.

I imagine a bright sun over the island in the sea and the plain and the foothills and the mountain. The sunlight covers all of them. This is the blessing of our teachers. This is the blessings of the holy beings who have brought this knowledge to us. They are the light of this world. This world would be dark without them. They have carefully, gently, with great tapas in their own lives, for thousands of years they have passed on these things from generation to generation. And you can always ask them for help: *ishvara pranidanadva.* There are many ways to reach what you need, but there's always an alternate. Just pray to the holy beings for help. They will help. So learn, think about what you've learned, meditate, and always pray for the blessings of the holy, beautiful beings who surround us. They will give it the more you believe.

Someone said they're going to hand out special strings today or tomorrow, I don't know, we call *sungdu. Sung* means "protection," *du* means a knotted string that you wear. This is supposed to protect you. If you get into an accident, you wouldn't get hurt so much. It's a piece of string. It doesn't have any power at all. The power comes from your faith. The power comes from your innocence and your hope. *That* protects you when you have a problem. I don't mean psychologically. I mean reality shifts because of your faith.

So for the first step of *tu sam gom sum,* you need a good teacher. Some teachers are good at explaining things. They know the path by head. Some teachers just experience things, and they know the path by foot. I think it's good to have a teacher who has both. So first you need a good, authentic teacher who knows how to explain what they have taken the hard work, the tapas, to actually experience.

Another powerful aid is *chulam gyi nelnjor.* We talked about it yesterday. It's the habit of stopping every ten or twenty minutes. We said you could make a secret sign that no one knows. Maybe you pull your ear, maybe you scratch your cheek, maybe you just chew on your fingernails. And then every time you do this secret sign, you believe that off to your right, behind a clear curtain, is all the living creatures in the whole universe who are hoping you will come for them. And you imagine that you are touching them and comforting them. And then you go back to your conversation with your friend.

I'd like to do a *chulam nelnjor* now. We had an agreement. Last night you knelt before your holy makeshift altar and you spoke out loud the secret sign. "I will make this sign, and then you people, suffering beings, beautiful living creatures will know I'm trying hard. I'm coming soon." So I'd like to ask everyone to close their eyes, because the signs are secret. Then make your sign and do your hour-to-hour yoga.

[Pause]

OK. And no longer than that. You could and you should do it constantly during the day, every time you remember. It's the first step in planting a powerful seed in your mind to be able to see those beings yourself.

I think the last preliminary is that it is very good to have a dharma friend, a spiritual friend, or two or three.

I don't think you fully appreciate who holy Lama Khen Rinpoche is, our root Lama. The traditional enrollment of the three great Gelukpa monasteries in Tibet was about 20,000 monks. There were many more at the two tantric colleges and many minor monasteries around Lhasa. Every year at the Munlam there would be public examinations of candidates to become a geshe. There are many kinds of geshes. The highest rank is *hlarampa*. There would be, oh say, two *hlarampas* from each monastery of five to eight thousand monks. Then those eight or nine *hlarampas* would be taken into the Potala palace where no one went. They would be set before His Holiness, the Dalai Lama. They would debate each other. One or two would be chosen *angi dangpo*. *Angi dangpo* means "highest rank."

Khen Rinpoche, holy lama, he achieved the highest of those ranks in the year he was examined. In the whole nation of Tibet, he was the greatest geshe. Then he became the administrator of Gyume Tantric College. There are only two Tantric colleges in Tibet. You have to be a *hlarampa* geshe even to ask to come. You only can apply after twenty-five or thirty years of intense study and practice. And he was the administrator. He was chosen as the head, to be the abbot after the next abbot resigned.

One day I asked him, "Rinpoche, how did you do it?"

He said, "Geshe Jampa Sengge."

45

I said, "Was he your teacher?"

He said, "No, he was my roommate."

"Who is he? Where is he now?"

"He's dead."

"Could you tell me about him?"

"He was a *bunpo*. He was a shaman. He was like a spiritual magician. He snuck into Sera, and posing as a monk he got ordained. He was intending to swipe the knowledge of the Buddhists and bring it back to the shamans of the mountains. He never went home."

Then he and Rinpoche ended up in the same room, and night after night in the dark they would talk about the lessons and their practice. And they would question each other relentlessly. And after twenty years of this they both got the highest rank in the same year. Geshe Jampa Sengge went to Italy later. He became the teacher of the great Giuseppe Tucci. And he passed away there.

But Rinpoche often said that the reason he went from a naughty young man to a holy lama was the exchange with a true friend. The bad friends take you to movies. The bad friends show you Time magazine. Bad friends waste your time with worthless hours of talk. Dharma friends try to discuss the holy things that are happening to them and you, and between the two of you, you get stronger and stronger. When you don't feel like meditating they force you. When you want to eat all the cookies off the altar, they stop you—unfortunately. This is a real dharma friend. And there's no better way to reach your goals than to find one or two.

Then you have to start a study of the great books. We live in a world full of books. There are thousands and thousands of books that come out every year. We pick up a book and we read it through and we put it down. And next year no one buys it anymore.

In the monastery, in the first twelve years you read one book, *Abhisamayalamkara* by Maitreya, the future Buddha. It's only fifty pages long, so you go through at an average of four pages per year. You debate it. You memorize it. You tear it apart, for, oh, twelve hours a day, fifteen hours a day. How could you do four pages a year like that? These are not books. These are holy, sacred, secret messages sent to us by Holy Beings, and they have withstood the test of time. Maybe every thousand years one of these books is released to us.

You have those books, frankly due to the kindness only of Khen Rinpoche and Geshe Thubten Rinchen and other great Lamas. And frankly due to the kindness of holy lama John Stilwell, who is sitting here, you have all of them ready, the eighteen courses, the five great books. Extremely rare, precious in this planet. You have all of them.

And due to the efforts of Khen Rinpoche's holy students, Lama Art, Dieter, Lolly, Maria, her husband, these holy people who have worked their whole lives, you have everything you need from the secret teachings as well. So don't waste your time on lesser things. We don't have much time.

I think it's good to take a break. Have a nice break. Smile at each other. When Winston-la rings the gong, please come back.

[Break.]

The next step of learning in the old way, which is the only way, is to memorize the instructions. And in the old days this was passed on from teacher to student orally. The teacher would sing a few lines, and the student would repeat, and then slowly they would memorize the book to be taught before they were allowed to learn what it meant. This is still the tradition.

Memorizing has got a bad name in the West. It's considered uncreative. Modern methods of education refuse any value in it. It is said that children who just memorize things don't learn what it really means and they can just end up being like parrots. But this is a very wrong idea, especially for holy books.

In the monastery, the first major book you would memorize is the book I mentioned by Lord Maitreya, the future Buddha. It was brought back to us by Lord Asanga, who met Maitreya in a buddha paradise and was taught it by memory.

I can't even begin to explain what it feels like to have Maitreya, a totally compassionate, holy, enlightened, omniscient being, whispering in your mind all day. It's

47

an unbelievable pleasure. It's an unbelievable comfort. Whenever you have a problem, whenever you're getting angry, whenever there's a difficult situation, Maitreya himself begins to whisper in your mind his holy lines. It's a companion for life.

These are not books. These are putting a Holy Being inside your head. In the strangest moments they come out and speak to you. It's a blessing to memorize. We were driving in a car, the retreatants and I, several years ago through a forest near Flagstaff. One of the retreatants in the back spat out, *"Chomdende!,"* which is *bhagavan.* It's in the beginning of the Heart Sutra.

And we turned around. "What?"

"I don't know. It just came." *[Laughs.]* It's a blessing. Oh, you have to do it. It's wonderful.

Choose the book carefully. It's hard to memorize things. It takes a long time to memorize even a few minutes of a book. I'll tell you the traditional ones. Maybe you'd like to try to start.

At first a person would learn the simple mantras: *om mani padme hum.* It was said in olden days there were people so thick that when they got to *"padme hum"* they forgot *"om mani,"* and when they got to *"om mani"* they forgot *"padme hum."* But with time, all of us can learn. Then the longer mantras, Vajrasattva's mantra for example.

Then, traditionally we would learn the prayers before our class—*Sashi Pukyi* [mandala offering] and prayers like that, *Sangye Chudang* [refuge and bodhichit-ta]. And the verse for dedicating goodness, *Gewa Diyi,* which comes from Arya Nagarjuna. Then a young boy in the monastery would learn the simple graces for offering the first part of our meals to holy beings. After that, almost always, *Ganden Hlagyama,* the Thousand Angels of the Heaven of Bliss. It's a meditation text, how to prepare for meditation by praying to the incomparable Je Tsongkapa.

After that, holy Lama Khen Rinpoche would make us learn *Lojong Tsig Gyema.* This is eight short verses written by Diamond Lion a thousand years ago to try to develop kindness. After that, one of the short lamrims, the instruction books for reaching enlightenment. There are only twelve to twenty verses. I think a great one to start is *Lam Tso Namsum*, "The Three Principal Paths." It's in the book called "Principal Teachings of Buddhism." Then *Yunten Shirgyurma*, "The Source of All my Good," which is in the book called "Preparing for Tantra." Or if you are ambitious, *Lamrim Duden*, "The Song of My Spiritual Life," by Je Tsongkapa. I think it's in the course on ethics.

Then the Heart Sutra is traditionally learned after that. And then even a young child, seven to eight, nine years old, would begin learning "The Ornament of Realizations" by Maitreya. It's about fifty pages. It takes thirty minutes to recite. Next would be the *Madhyamika Avatara*, "Entering the Middle Way," by Chandrakirti. This takes longer, maybe forty-five, fifty minutes. Next the *Abhidharmakosha* by Master Vasubandhu, "The Treasure of Higher Knowledge." It's over an hour, maybe an hour and fifteen minutes.

Not too many people make it through all the Five Great Books, frankly. Most of them forget them quickly after they reach America. But next would be *Vinaya Sutra*, on how to live a good life, rules for monks and nuns. This takes close to two hours. And a few brave souls memorize the *Pramanavartika* of Dharmakirti on logic and perception. And that is difficult. It also takes over an hour.

A very few, maybe two or three a year of the best monks will then undertake to memorize the entire *Drange Lekche Nyingpo*. This is 230 pages long, and it explains the difference between the Mind Only school and the Middle Way school. Holy Lama Winston has kindly worked much of his life for the last few years to prepare transcripts and to organize and edit the teachings which we were so fortunate to receive from Geshe Thubten Rinchen-hla, holy lama, on this same book.

After that, if a student were fortunate enough to meet a tantric master, they would start to memorize their prayers for their secret meditations. These are sadhanas, *dakkye*. And if you have been fortunate enough to have been granted one, which happens to about one person in a million, you should certainly try to memorize parts, and then eventually the whole thing. Imagine having an enlightened, holy beautiful woman whispering in your ear all day long.

Don't be a fool. Don't think those are long, boring prayers. Keep it precious in your heart. Learn it.

Oh, I wanted to say, it doesn't have to be in Tibetan. The Tibetans don't memorize it in Sanskrit any more, do they? *[Laughs.]* But according to your capacity, if you can learn the Tibetan, and memorizing is a great way to learn, try. If not, English is wonderful. If you're ambitious, at the end of everything go and memorize the Sanskrit versions. Some people have.

Also it's a great help to others. When you're teaching—and all of you must teach—you can speak with authority. This is very important for people who want to learn holy knowledge from you. They can be confident that you're not just making up something. They can be confident that they are receiving instructions that have been spoken by an enlightened Being who has explained everything. So even for the sake of your disciples, your own students, start now.

I would like to talk a little bit about how to memorize. I think it's very important. No one taught me properly. I sat on the edge of my bed with a book for years and struggled. Then I had the honor to stay in a small room on top of Sera Mey main temple. And I saw a holy lama named Geshe Lobsang Pende in the dusk. He was pacing on the roof from wall to wall, from the parapet. He looked like, you know, those Olympic swimmers who swim fast and long and dive down and kick and return. And he had his rosary behind him and he was bent over and he was speeding towards the wall.

I almost yelled, "Geshe-hla, don't bang your head, or fall off!" And then he would suddenly turn around and come back. And then they taught me: walk. Walk when you memorize. It's very powerful. It keeps your channels open and it refreshes your mind. Walk in a circle in your yurt or between two places, but walk. I find it very nice to do under trees.

Then, start small. Everybody who tries to start to memorize expects to recite the *Lamrim Chenmo* in a week. It doesn't work that way. The great lamas, Je Tsong-kapa, would memorize ten or twenty pages a day their whole life. We can't do that. You start with a small prayer, four lines, and try to make a goal, maybe a line every three or four days. And don't be discouraged. When you're first starting, this is very, very normal. Everyone's like that. When you get to the second line, you'll forget the first line. It's OK. Everyone is like that.

The ability to memorize increases as you get more practice. You have to do it steadily, every single day, and only five or ten minutes. Don't do more; you'll quit. Just five or ten minutes. Take that one prayer, the short verse, and recite it three times. The first time, look at the book or the paper while you're walking. The second time, close the paper and go as far as you can without looking. Then open it up and finish. Then go through one third time, one more time, looking at the paper. Three times, and then just stop.

There's a secret to memorizing. After about, oh, five minutes are past and you've finished the three times through, then close the paper and just walk and think about the meaning of what you've memorized. Go through like one line on the first day and think carefully about the meaning. And the next day, go to the second line, and so on. This prevents you from becoming one of those mechanical parrots, which you do meet in the monastery, who never understand what they've memorized.

I'll tell you another common danger. People finally make it through their first little prayer, and they're so excited that they've mastered it, and they go to the second one right away. Don't do that. After you've finished a whole book or prayer, then keep on it every day for half the time it took you to memorize it. If it took you eight month to memorize a small book, then spend four months more just getting used to it. Don't jump to the next book right away.

There's an instruction in your book. It says, "Sing-along beads." In the monastery, the young men go out in the evening to sing their memorizing. It's so beautiful. Those of you who went to Sera, I think you heard them. And one of the most lovely things is that, being refugees, they come from all parts of Tibet. And they sing in the song of their own region. And it's very beautiful to hear. The Khampas will say, "*adikeya adackia aduppa achikdena,*" and then the Utsang will say, "*dikke dakki duppa duchikna,*" and the Amdowas will say, "*dikkay dakkee dubaw achiknena.*" And the Tre'o Khampas, who no one can understand, "*waddyka wadaka washmema…*"

And they all have their own song. It's very beautiful. We are the pioneers now in America. We can put them to our own songs. I know one venerable chanting master who is doing this. I think it's wonderful. I'm doing mine to Neil Young. Don't be shy. Don't be embarrassed. This is your right, to find the most beautiful song you like and use it.

I heard such beautiful music. We were sent some beautiful CDs from a holy yoga center in New York. Some *kirtan* singing. It's very beautiful. It would go very well with many of our prayers. Other people sent us *qualli* music, the Islam, holy

51

singers. These are also very beautiful tunes. You can choose your own. Don't be shy. You don't have to sound Tibetan. They don't sing in Sanskrit. They use their own beautiful songs of their country.

It's helpful to carry some beads. You can knock off a bead for every verse, or every line. If you tend to get lost you can count the beads and see if there's still multiples of four.

The text you have says, "Watch for holes." This has three meanings. First is literal. If you're on the roof *[laughs]*, if you're pacing on a roof then be careful and don't step off the side. You can get excited and step on a rattlesnake or something. With a little bit, you have to watch where you're going.

The second meaning of "watch for holes" is after you've memorized something and then six months have passed, your mind tends to change it. Like all the rock and roll songs I knew a century ago, and I sing them to myself silently sometimes, and sometimes I hear the original and the words have changed. So it's good to go back to the original at times and check yourself. Make sure you're still doing it purely. It's a very strict responsibility and custom in our lineage that you never change the original. Never. You memorize it exactly as it was spoken by the first guru thousands of years ago. It's a very wrong thing to corrupt a text or add things. These are instructions given by enlightened, holy beings. We can't mess around with them. We will destroy them for future people.

The third meaning of "watch for holes" is very serious. The greatest memorizer in the time of Lord Buddha was Devadatta, his half-brother who hated Lord Buddha and tried to compete with him in everything. He could recite thousands and thousands of pages of scripture, out of pride and out of a sense of competition. Envy. Wanting to appear knowledgeable, more than his half-brother. And all of us are susceptible to the same thing. All of us, without exception, are susceptible to pride about things we've learned. And so you have to be very careful. This is a great danger the more you learn. You have to be very, very careful. It will bring great suffering to you and others if you allow pride to infect your learning. And it will, and we have to try and fight against it.

"Return at times" means go back after you've memorized it, oh, every week, and do the old things. Otherwise they slip away. "Use your time" means memorizing is a wonderful way to use your spare time, what I like to call "waste time."

I use drive Holy Lama to Washington, D.C., once a month. It's a four-, five-hour drive. So why not recite the *Abhisamayalamkara* five or six times on the way? And this is very wonderful way to use your time. We are often made to wait for others. We often have times during the day when we have to sit somewhere. And use the time. You'll even see the holy young monks like Jampa while as they cook or do other duties they will sing their songs to themselves. It's a wonderful way to spend the time with meaning.

A word of warning: everything you memorize you will forget. It happens to everyone. Lamas often say to you, "I've forgotten more text than you've ever memorized." Be graceful. It's part of the process. You can't recite twenty-five hours of text every day. The effect is the important thing. It will stay in your mind singing. The repercussions of it will sing in your consciousness for many lifetimes.

I studied with a holy Lama, Geshe Ngawang Kelden, in New Jersey. He lived in the Buxa refugee camp. He was from Inner Mongolia. He was studying in Tibet when it was invaded. He reached India. He lived in the jungle there. Like half the monks there, he got tuberculosis. He was cut open. They cut out a lung. He would walk around the temple in New Jersey bent over on his side, wheezing and taking tiny steps. When he taught you, you had to wait a few minutes between each line.

He was on his deathbed. I saw him reading a book. I said, "Geshe-hla, what is it?"

He said, "*Dura, dura yin.* I'm studying primary logic," the thing that twelve, fifteen-year-old children study in the monastery.

I couldn't believe it. I said, "Geshe-hla, at a time like this, why?"

He said, "Nothing is lost. I'm putting it in my heart."

So, and then he died *[crying]*. So nothing is lost. Don't worry if you forget things.

I know some of you are thinking, "It's too late for me. I'm already too old to do this sort of thing."

It's never too late. That's a foolish idea. Five or ten minutes a day to have the honor of Maitreya whispering to you.

53

Then go for teachings on the book you've learned. In your text it says, I think, "Swim in the pool." Teachings are like a huge ocean. You can never learn all of them. But the process of being exposed to them constantly will give you the ability to see the things we spoke about.

"Sip the nectar four times." It means when you hear a teaching once, then try to review it three times afterwards. This is an ancient custom. Don't go back to the second day of teaching until you've gone over the first day three times. It doesn't have to be formal. It could be on your way home tonight in a car. And you just decide to think about it for twenty minutes.

Then "lock it in a crystal jar." In Tibet, learning, listening to a teaching was considered a grave action, because after that you are responsible for handing it on to the next person. Many people would refuse to go to a teaching because they knew of this responsibility and it was too serious for them. It's our responsibility to pass this light on to the next generation. Otherwise everything will become dark in this world. People will believe you can't see what's going to happen after you die. People will believe your mind can't see every world and every human, animal living there. People will believe there are no angels around us. The world will be thrown into a very terrible darkness. Our country is close to that.

The people here have worked very hard. I've seen beautiful records of teachings given in the last few years, put out by the usual anonymous do-gooders who refuse to put their names on things.

Many of the people here have worked very hard, and we are very grateful. We receive books of holy Lama Khen Rinpoche's teachings, which have been prepared by his devout holy students, disciples, who are great lamas themselves. We have received holy books of holy Lama Zopa Rinpoche's teachings. They are like, oh, a beautiful meal for us during our break times. The people in charge of ACI have been kind enough to send us, expensive, a complete set of all the tapes and texts. We use them constantly during our break month. This is a very kind thing to do for us and for others. And there are other people here who are making beautiful transcriptions of secret teachings, constantly.

So keep it for others. And "cherish the flower." Every time you get a chance to thank someone, a teacher or one of the holy disciples who have recorded things for us, passed them to us, then thank them and be joyful. They're so rare. So often, I know because I have this problem, we tend to be competitive with other traditions or other teachers or other groups. But if we can cherish each tradition and learn from it, it's a precious thing. There's too little holy learning in this country. Every little piece is precious. Every little kind holy thing that someone can try to do is another step for us all. And if you have time you should learn those.

If you are attracted to the Christian path then you should memorize the words of Jesus. If you are attracted to the holy path of ancient India you should memorize the holy books, the Bhagavad Gita and Yoga Sutras. If you are attracted to the Judaic path then you should memorize the great books of the ancient prophets. Every kind thing that happens is *sanggye kyi trinle yin kyappey chir,* it's an activity of equally enlightened beings in this world. We have to, we're very lucky every time someone turns any wheel of any dharma. There's so little.

The second stage after learning is contemplation. This is after you've taken a teaching you go home and you think about it. In silence you mull it over to yourself. Then after that, when you're with others, try to turn the conversation to holy talk. It's hard. There's a great wave of useless talk slashing from coast to coast constantly. It's hard to fight against it. But as you sit with others, then question each other.

There's a great danger—I know because I wasted many years of my precious life being jealous or competitive with my fellow holy students—but if you can break through that then you drop your pride and your envy and you say to someone in a car, "What do you think about that *pratyaksha* thing? And that *agama*? Seems to me it's just another kind of *anumana.*" And start a conversation like that.

When I first got to New Jersey there were, oh, ten refugee Mongolian monks, and Khen Rinpoche and myself and holy Lama Art, and I remember they would assemble for prayers. We would drink tea together at their table and try to listen to their holy talk. And there was a great *hlarampa* from Kalmykia, the last of the great Kalmyk lamas. His name was Geshe Ngawang Yampel. He was blind. He had had a cataract operation. They told him to leave the bandages on for four or five days. He tore them off and started reading his scriptures. Then he went blind. But he was a great master.

Then there was Geshe Kalden and *hlarampa* Geshe Khen Rinpoche. And Geshe Kalden was funny. He would sit there at tea and very humbly ask one of the great geshes a question. We couldn't figure it out. We knew he knew the answer already. But he just wanted to hear it said again. It takes great humility to ask a question of your fellow students. It's a good practice. You might even learn something new.

So get over these demons of laziness and pride and envy and question each other, like the old Socrates, the old Greeks. And debate. Debate is a very beautiful custom. I'm not talking about two politicians getting up and exchanging unkind remarks. In the old days, ever since thousands of years ago, the great wise men would sit together and they would question each other. In ancient India it was called *satsang*. The custom continues to today, even with great American and other Western teachers of ancient Indian traditions. It's a beautiful thing to see. And you ask questions, and you sit quietly in the evening and enjoy holy talk.

In Tibet and in ancient India, this custom became formalized into great formal debates. You've seen them. You've seen pictures. Some of you have been to Sera. And it has become a very exciting exploration. People purposely sit together. They gather in a group of maybe ten or fifteen fellow students. One student sits at the head of the circle, another student or two jumps up and races towards them and screams a question at the top of their lungs. And claps their hands and dances in a circle. This is a beautiful exciting way to learn. In a single evening you can learn more than months of classes. And the great debaters always explore the questions they're not sure of. The wimpy debaters explore the questions they figured out last year, because they don't want to appear to not understand something. The great debaters bring up the questions they don't know about. It can be a very exciting, beautiful process. I think we should have it here, or wherever we end up.

Before you go into a debate you have to prepare your weapons. There's a beautiful story in Tibet. *"Kyakpa tang sa la menda le, menda gyap sa la kyakpa le."* A guy was on his way to the front lines to fight a battle. There's a joke in Tibet: "A major battle took place in Kham yesterday. Three people got hurt." Anyway. He stopped at a farmhouse on the way to the front lines for the night. In Tibet it was a custom to put up any traveler for free and feed them. He went to the outhouse with his rifle, and he left it there. Next day he walked on to the front lines. He ran into the enemy. He reached for his rifle and he realized it was gone, in the outhouse. And so he crapped in his pants out of fear. And he asked the enemy if he could wait while he ran and got his gun.

56

So it means he left his gun where you shoot your poop, and he left his poop where you should shoot your gun. And in Tibet in means you walk into a debate without being ready. You have to prepare two things.

In the text it says, "Jampa." Many of you know the greatest lama in America is the anonymous cook in New Jersey, pretending to be a normal guy. Perfect service of his lama. Perfect heart. His last name Lungrik. *Lung* means "scripture, *agama.*" *Rik* means "*rigpa,* logic." When you enter a debate you have to be armed with what you've memorized because no papers are allowed in the debate ground. And you have to have logic. You have to be able to follow a logical flow.

Logic has a bad name in America. Logic is boring. Logic is syllogisms. People say logic doesn't work to get you to mystical goals. They use logic to prove how logic is not necessary, without being aware of it. We use logic constantly: driving a car, walking from the parking lot here. When you frame a sentence you use count-less shades of logic to order the words properly. Speech, thinking, is logic itself. It's a path to mystical experiences. So when you go into a debate you have to be logical. If in a debate you're not logical, even since ancient times, they would just throw you out. You follow a path or reasoning. You reach the truth. Your feeling when you debate with your fellows has to be, "we are searching for the truth."

People came with me to the geshe examinations. They would watch from behind a wall as I was grilled. And then afterwards they would race up and say, "Who won?" And the Tibetans couldn't understand the question. It's not the point; they don't even think about it. It's an exploration for the truth. If you have a good heart, if you try hard, if you sit down with your fellow dharma students and reach over the wall of envy and pride, you will both come to the truth. Oftentimes young debaters will debate a question the whole night, and then maybe a week later will find the answer in a book that you all came up with already. This is true explora-tion. This is how to get true knowledge.

The second meaning of "Jampa," his name means "love, *maitri.*" You can't be a successful debater, you can't explore the real meaning of truth, if you don't have love. In my class in Sera we started with sixty monks. I was awed at the begin-ning. They were fifteen, twenty years younger than me and they were so good. And they had memorized everything, and they could debate everything. I could hardly follow them the first few years. Some seemed very prideful. Some seemed very gentle. At the end of the course, almost twenty years later, there were only three monks left. It was all the gentle ones. It was all the kind ones. So when you debate, go around the table, see who's lost. See who's afraid to speak. See who's not confident. And purposely help them, engage them, find out what they know. Find out what they can contribute. Don't ignore them. Don't leave them. And this love is what will make you successful in finding truth. That's why the text says, "Have Jampa hold your gun."

We have a tiny bit more to go. I think you need some more refreshments. I'm sorry it's long. Please have something to drink or snack. After that, it's very short.

[Break.]

I wanted to emphasize, when I say logic I mean questioning, whether it's in your own mind or sitting around with coffee and a few good dharma friends and just asking each other the questions that you're wondering about. It's a beautiful way to use the faculty of speech. Then you come to some sort of conclusions. For example, after tomorrow's talk I think you'll have all the information you need to actually see those things we spoke about—what's going to happen to you in the very end of things. You'll come to be able to see all the beings there are, all their worlds, in a single moment. And you'll make contact and be taken care of by holy beings, like angels. And you'll see their essence.

These things happen in a state of deep meditation. All the learning, all the memorizing, all the classes, all the teachings, all the questioning, is only preparation. The real thing takes place in deep meditation. So I think it's important to say that for every hour you study, or learn, or memorize, or debate, or question, or contemplate, you must spend one hour in deep meditation. It's a rule of thumb. And I know on behalf of all the retreatants, we beg you not to abuse this guideline. And especially not for us. We don't want that karma. You take care of your meditations and your retreats. We can take a little less of whatever we need. You make sure you use your time in the right priority. It's a very holy deed to serve people in retreat, but not if you're not meditating yourself.

We hear rumors of many people in retreat. It's a great joy for us. People who didn't have time before are making time. They are doing one month retreats. We're very happy when we hear. We feel you in retreat. We don't have special powers; I don't. I should say, I don't claim on behalf of all us to be able to read anyone's minds or anything like that. But I can say that we sense you in retreat, even in the East Coast. We are very happy.

We have six senses by which we can experience *pratyaksha*, direct perception of things. We can see beautiful things. We can hear directly. We can smell directly the occasional pizza. *[Laughs.]* That's not a hint. We can taste. We feel the touch of the air and clothing. And we have a capacity of direct mental perception. When you remember an object, you're having a direct perception—in the higher schools. When you hear yourself talking to yourself in your mind, you're having a direct perception. The mind of a moment before is serving up something for the mind of the present moment to hear. These are direct perceptions.

There's a seventh direct perception. It is taught in the scriptures on perception and logic. It's called *nelnjor ngunsum*. *Nelnjor* means "yoga;" *ngunsum* means "direct perception." It means that in a state of deep meditation a person who has been trained properly by study, by thinking, by questioning, and by having a good heart and thinking about all the suffering they can help stamp out, then in an incredible moment of deep meditation you can directly see what you will become in the end, the savior of countless living creatures in our world. Each of you will become. You don't have to take my word for it. You can see it. Imagine what it feels like to look into the future and see yourself helping millions of living creatures. Imagine how it feels. You will. You can see it. Imagine what it feels like to look upon countless planets, see countless precious, holy, suffering, little ones, and know you will help them. All in a few minutes time.

Imagine what it's like to make your first contact with an angel and speak with them. Imagine what it's like to see the real reality that lies above this one. You can do it. You have to meditate. After all the other preparation, you are ready. You have something to meditate about. Don't be a fool and sit down without it ready. You need to prepare for the meditation. You need to have something to meditate on. That was the purpose of learning and thinking, years of work. Then sit down. That's the most important instruction there is. Sit still. It's so hard for us. Find a silent place. This place is hot. This place is freezing. This place is dangerous with snakes and other animals. This place is lonely. But this place is quiet.

It's important to, if you can, get out of the cities, get away from the towns, if you really want to meditate deeply. The cars make subtle vibrations throughout the earth. The radios and televisions send vibrations through your body. The emotions of a million people or more wash over you. And the noises of your house, electrical appliances, the people talking… I'm not saying you can't see these things in your own home. You can. That's true. You will, you can. But the quieter place you can find, the better your chances.

Then your body has to be silent. It takes, actually, a great deal of physical strength to sit quietly for even half an hour. It looks like it doesn't take any strength. It takes a lot of strength of your body to sit still and straight for even half an hour. If your backbone and the channels which run close to it are not aligned and straight, you can't meditate properly. You certainly can't undertake the more advanced practices. And so it's very important to keep your body healthy and to exercise it wisely, without vanity. I think yoga is a very ancient way and a good way, the *asana* exercises. And these have a great effect on your channels. We have been very honored as retreatants to have several very amazing and qualified teachers to help us.

And thirdly, your mind must be silent. *[Laughs.]* After a year and a half of silence, we are all very sensitive. We know each bird's song. We sing them to each other and laugh. But there is this tremendous noise of our own minds talking all day. It almost makes you crazy. It's hard to stop.

The text says, "*Tatsta tadanjanata samapati.*" *Tatsta* means "keep the mind fixed on the object." Fixation is the first goal. It's done by stopping the mind from wandering away. The greatest single method for this is sadness. Even if you find yourself distracted or unable to get quiet, driving around, then think about all of us. We are all half-dead. We are all dying. We are all scratching at the earth as the huge snake devours us. All our efforts of our whole lifetimes will be erased in a few years after we die. Our situation is hopeless. Out of millions and millions of people we have a tiny chance of success to escape. It's a very serious and sad war. It will immediately bring your mind down, *tatsta.*

Tadanjanata means you need "clarity." Clarity doesn't mean the clearness of the object. It means the sharpness and brightness of your own mind, bright eyed and bushy tailed, the way you feel when you're reading a great book or listening to Neil Young. The mind is bright, the mind is engaged, the mind is into it, maybe you're even slobbering. That's *tadanjanata*. It's the opposite of *jingwa. Jingwa* means the mind gets dull, the mind zones out, the mind spaces out. These are the two great extremes, which destroy meditation. Either you are thinking about lunch, wandering, or you are spaced out, the mind is dull, you ate too much. How many meditation sessions have we, have I given up before they started by eating the wrong things before, or not sleeping well.

Samapati means you reach a state of balance. In Tibetan it's called *nyampar jokpa*. *Nyampar* means "balance." *Jokpa* means you reached a state in your meditation. This is how to make your mind silent. You don't need a lot of instructions. If the mind is wandering, think of all of us. Who will die next? If the mind is zoned out, think of how lucky we are, one in a million to have a little chance. We are like the little rabbit that was saved.

Become a master not only of the subject of your meditation. Pay attention to the method, master the process, become a serious hard-ass *tapas*-oriented meditator. Learn all the details of meditation. You have the (ACI) Course Three from holy Kamalashila: *Bhavanakarma*, "The Stages of Meditation," and you have the unbelievable chart by the teacher of His Holiness, the incomparable Trijang Rinpoche. Study it, learn it, learn the preliminaries and learn the problems that will come up in meditation.

One of the teachers who comes in to help us, keep our bodies working and keep our channels open, blurted out, "Oh, I saw such and such a caretaker teaching this unbelievable course on meditation—the five problems, the eight antidotes." We were so happy to hear it.

Become a master not only of the object, but pay attention to the method of meditating. And then constantly improve it. Don't be lazy. Don't just flop down and try to wander. I have found it useful, once a week on Monday, I think of it like a high jumper. Raise the bar. Once a week raise the bar. Make your goal a little higher. It means if you're only able to sit quietly for fifteen minutes without moving, then on Monday, every Monday, raise the bar. How much? It's not what you expect. It's harder than you think. Raise it by one minute. I'm not kidding. One minute a week is a wonderful achievement, but be steady. In one year you will be totally quiet, silent, unmoving for an hour. It's beautiful. It's enough. One year is not much time to spend for that. Don't do more. "I'm on 28 minutes this week," and then stick it out. Stay totally unmoving.

If you can, learn some of the meditation postures from a qualified teacher. Some of the yoga teachers who are so kind to help us are very good at teaching this. See if you can stay in, say, a full lotus for, oh, three minutes, and then four minutes.

61

Raise the bar every Monday.

Around the tenth week, one of your children will get sick. There will be a disaster with the water tank. One of those dumb retreatants will get bitten again, and then you'll fall back. You'll get into a rhythm, and then things happen. Face it, it happens all the time. You go ten weeks, you're up to eleven minutes without moving. I know some of the retreatants who track their mind not moving. "I got twelve minutes in on the object today. Man!" It's a lot.

So things will happen, your rhythm, your progress will be stopped, you'll drop. Then circle back like an army in retreat, and come back to the front and start again. If you were up to fifteen minutes without moving an eyelash and you got interrupted for a week by one of those world disasters, then come back at twelve minutes and start working up again, but be relentless. What I'm trying to say is in memorizing, in study, in debating, in meditation, you're going to have obstacles. You will drop. Something will happen. All of the progress you made for a few weeks will be stopped. Then just come back gracefully, patiently, persistently and start again, oh, five to ten minutes less than before. And within a year or two you'll be a great meditator.

It's only in the deepest meditation that you can get a direct experience. It's like having an eye in your own heart, and the eye suddenly opens, and without moving, with your eyes, your physical eyes closed you see the future. You see what you will be. You can't describe how it feels, and how many people you can help.

And I want to emphasize, as we stop, that it's impossible if you don't do it for others. It will never happen. You have to look at the people around you. Stop worrying about yourself. Everything will be taken care of if you take care of others. They are dying. Almost no one in this country knows what's going on with themselves. They are in a hopeless state. They are worse that the baby, the child rabbit. They can't even cry out. There's no one to cry to.

It's an unspoken truth of our lives. We are just headed for our death. It's obvious that all the great works of people are nothing more than a baby rabbit scratching in the dirt. They disappear in about the same speed. You can help them. You have to help them. Each person becomes the savior of their own world. It's a wonderful idea; it's true. Each of you will become the one who saves the other people here. It's a trick of emptiness.

That's all.

Tonight add something to your secret signs. There's a certain stage called *chu gyun kyi ting nge dzin*. In deep meditation before you see the other things, you are able to travel back in time. It's not like the other things I spoke about. It's a different process. You follow back the seeds in your mind. You look at one seed in your mind and you follow the thread back to the seed that caused that one. And then you follow that seed back..

Samskara sakshat karanat purvajati jnanam, in the text. You follow your *sams-karas*, your *bakchaks*, back. You know, "When did I first have this thought about this thing? What planted that thought five years before that? What came before? How did I have that thought? When is the first time in my life I can remember having a thought like this?" You can follow the *bakchaks* back, only in deep medi-tation. It's not a direct perception like those other ones, but you can learn to follow back the threads. *Chugyun* means the threads of what you've known and learned. *Ting nge dzin* means *samadhi*, deep concentration.

If you follow back far enough you will come across the holy teacher who taught you before you came to this world. It's impossible that you or I got this far without the direct guidance of great gurus and lamas before. It could have been on other worlds. It could be that they didn't look anything like Tibetan or Indian teachers of this time or this world. They could have been totally different. There are many worlds where the great teachers are all women of knowledge. It could have been someone like that, but you can go back and find them and see them. They can certainly see you.

So it's a very holy practice to do a *chulam gyi nelnjor* with them. I suggest tonight you create a second secret sign. You speak it out loud. They don't need the speak-ing out loud. It's for us. You say, "When I put my hand on my shoulder and reach back behind to the past, or when I rub my neck, as if I were trying to do a certain yoga exercise and messed it up again, then it's a sign that I'm thinking of you, my sweet, holy, beautiful teacher who helped me come to this world. And please touch me sometime. Come and touch my hand."

Imagine their hand is close. They are very happy you are asking. Finally you recognize that they existed, and they touch your hand. It's a wonderful yoga. It's a wonderful secret practice.

So announce your sign tonight, kneeling before your altar. You now have the two yogas. Practice them all day, every ten or fifteen minutes just reach up to your shoulder. Imagine this holy lama, maybe a woman, touching your hand, and then bring it back to the present. This plants a seed to see them again.

Fourth Day:

Sunday, September 23, 2001

IV.

Throughout history,
Only the very good
Have seen.
Why?

Because there is nothing seen,
And there is nothing unseen.
There is no dark world,
There are no mists,
No shore, no highlands, no peaks:
The edges are impossible

No innocence,
Nothing to learn,
Nothing to contemplate,
Nothing on which to meditate.
The seed grows the flower
And the plant tags along.

Nothing is hidden,
Nothing revealed;
And you cross from one to the other
By sitting very still—
The mountain comes to you.

For we are workmen

Laying down path stones,
Then walking on them:
We lay down the dark,
We lay down the dim image,
We lay down the two true images,
And we lay down the solid object.

Our minds organize an image
Of an image as an image;
And our minds organize an image
Of an object as an object.
Don't confuse the two,
And don't think they're not real.

We are painters,
Painting each scene,
Then stepping into it
As we paint ourselves there.

It was never any other way;
This itself is Their very care.
Reach out to the left
To the light of a Diamond Sun.

Know though
That powerful hands move our own;
One thing decides pen or stick to chew on,
One thing decides the far and here,
The long away or now,
Lonely death or the company of Angels,
And that is kindness.

How kind? What edge?
How far from tongue to stomach?
How far too far?
How different too different?
How long ahead too long?

Do you expect me to feel responsible for people on worlds
that neither I nor others have ever seen; for those
who won't even be born for ten months or ten years
or ten thousand years?
Yes, it's what you are here to do;
And they are not unseen, nor unborn.
Reach ahead to the one who sees you,
Reach out to yourself.

First I'd like to really apologize for going so long yesterday. I didn't realize the time. And today I'd know a lot of you have long journeys to make. We'll finish without going too long.

First I'd like to meditate a minute.

Every person, every one of us, has two kinds of energies in us. One is a man's energy, and the other is a woman's energy, and each of us has both. They travel in special channels throughout our body that we can't see. One of them is much stronger than the other.

As you form in your mother's womb, the channels form, the energy starts moving in the channels, and then your body forms like clay around the channels. Depending on which energy is stronger, male or female, the clay forms into a man's body or a woman's body. But, as you go through your practices, and especially in the higher teachings, secret teachings, then the two energies begin to flow equally, within you. Then the clay starts to reform as a result, and if we can practice very well, then our body changes later in life, and it becomes like light.

Those bodies of beings of light don't have any sign of man or woman. They are inside of them both together a whole, like in union all the time. Both the energies are equal, and they flow into each other and combine. And the feeling of that is as if inside of one person a man and a woman were making love all the time within a single person. They feel that way constantly. And those bodies don't have any stomach or heart or lungs; they are pure light. Outwardly otherwise, they look like us, but all the pieces are made of light. When it is useful, they will send an image of a body to different places to teach people. I thought it was good to mention. I think it could be disconcerting to feel the energies becoming equal within you, but it's something very holy, and it's something to look forward to.

In the meantime, we are in a very hard desperate deadly place, which is called the desire realm, the realm of desire. His Holiness the First Dalai Lama says this is called the realm of desire because people are very attracted to solid hard things like food; people are very much attached to gross pleasures like sexual activity. And the beings here in our realm, we very much identify with the predominant energy. We think, "I am a man" or "I am a woman." And then we feel a strong attachment to the energy in another person. And so some people are attracted to a man's energy, and they feel comfortable around men. And other people, men or women, feel attracted to woman's energy, and they feel comfortable around women.

In my lifetime, we've been lucky to see a pattern changing. This used to be a whole civilization that was dominated by men's energy. Even back ten, fifteen thousand years, in the ancient culture of Indo-Europeans, and the other great culture which is our source, the Hebrew culture, it was a man's energy. The name for god was "Sky Father"—Ju Pitr. And that custom had passed down for many thousands of years—the man's energy stronger. There are something like four-and-a-half thousand exquisite beautiful texts in our ancient canon. Of those four-and-a-half thousand ancient books, which are the ancient core of our lineage, I believe there's only two or three which were spoken by women.

But in our days we are so lucky, times are changing. For example, we can now have a choice, if we want to go to a physician, a doctor, we can go to a man or a woman. It wasn't that way when I was younger. And many of us, myself included, feel more comfortable with a woman physician. I appreciate the gentleness and the sincerity. Some people equally feel comfortable with a man's energy; they like a man doctor who will speak with firmness and decisiveness, and a man's approach. And if half the people in our country would feel more comfortable with a woman teacher, or a woman lama, or a woman guru, then I think the time has come.
Those whose bodies have a woman's energy for now should prepare themselves. And I think here in Diamond Mountain, and in the retreat, and in the teaching by the caretakers and other people, women lamas are coming forth. It's a joy to see because you know that many people will be attracted to their energy, and more people will be happy, and comfortable to learn from them. And it's good to see

here so many people whose energy is woman's for now are serious and do deep retreats, studying hard.

I would like to just express my happiness and beg you to prepare yourselves. The time will come quickly when people will come to you. They will need your help. And it's not enough just to be a woman. People don't go to a woman physician just because she's a woman. It is important to them that she is, but they also want a good doctor. If the woman hasn't been trained well, if she can't really cure people, then the people won't come. But if she has taken many years of hard work to take her woman's energy, the sweet energy, and then train it, direct it, with hard work, hard studies, hard meditations, then she is a complete doctor for the people who would like to come to her. So I ask you, those whose energy for now is stronger woman's energy, get ready, work hard. I think this place is a good place for that.

We've been talking about things you can see and things you can't see. The things we can't see are very much more important. Where did we really come from? What are we supposed to do while we're here? What will we be like in the end? What are we growing into? If you could see those things, you could really help people. It's what everyone needs to know. It's what everybody wants to know. And you can do it; you can see it. People have done it.

What kind of people?

We see in our history, the short, very, very short history that we know about, it seems like only very good people, very special people get to see these things. We have a record of Moses, holy Moses, and he met a divine being. It has become almost just a legend. People aren't sure if he really did. There are stories in the Bible about Jesus telling his disciples about his death. They rebuke him. They say, "Don't talk like that. People will get scared." He seems to have seen the future, but this has also become like a legend. Most people don't really believe it.

We have many, many stories of the early Indian saints meeting divine beings. We have many accounts in the scriptures of Lord Buddha and his disciples seeing the future. There are stories of Lord Buddha going to other worlds to teach his parents who had died. People take these to be legends. We have records of Je Tsongkapa 600 years ago meeting with angels, especially Manjushri, and studying with them. It's extremely hard to believe that a normal human being could in one life, and not a very long life, compose ten thousand pages of scripture. Every single page is extraordinary. Every single page is more than the equal of Shakespeare, Aristotle, Einstein. It seems hard to believe he wasn't coached by a divine being, but again, it's like a legend.

There's a story of the Thirteenth Dalai Lama, His Holiness, who ordained holy Lama Khen Rinpoche. There's a very heartbreaking letter, a public letter, which he wrote thirty to forty years before Tibet was lost, describing how it would be lost, exactly, if people didn't change. All of these people had one thing in common. Moses' meeting with a divine being, I think, may have been the most important few minutes in the history of our civilization. He was presented with a list of actions. And the list was a list about not harming other people, and that list has become the core of whatever civilized behavior we are capable of.
Jesus was constantly talking about being kind to others, treating them like you would yourself. And the same message was the constant concern of the great saints of India, Lord Buddha, Je Tsongkapa, His Holiness the Thirteenth Dalai Lama. Why is it that only good people get to see the future? Why is it that only good people get to meet angels or holy beings? To understand this, I think you have to understand emptiness.

We spoke about five different frames of mind that you'll go through in your journey to see the events of the future and in your attempt to see all the living beings there are. We compared it to going from an island, to an ocean, to a great dry land, to the foothills of a mountain, and then on to the mountain.

I would like to speak about the emptiness of this process. We don't have much time; it's something you should think about later. You can read the little text, and maybe later get a tape or transcript, because it's a little bit hard, but try to think where are the edges between things. Where are the edges between things? Where does the island stop and the water begin? Where is the line or the edge between the water and the dry land? Where do the foothills start, exactly; what's the line? Where is the edge of the foothills, and where do the mountains start?

There are big trees here, I think oak trees. Look at the trees. Look at the sky around the top of the trees. Where does the tree stop and the sky begin? Where is the edge between the tree and the sky? Where does the tree touch the sky? Then your mind says very quickly, easily, "Oh, it's at the very edge."

What's the very edge look like?

"Oh, it's where the very tip of the tree touches the very tip or the edge of the sky. It's where the two colors touch."

How big is the place where the two colors touch?

"Oh, it's tiny. It's the very edge of the blue and the very edge of the green."

How tiny is the edge?

"It's tiny; it's as fine as a line."

Can you see the edge?

"Yes, I can."

So it has some thickness to it; if it didn't have thickness, you couldn't see it, right?

You say, "Right!"

So it's not the real edge, is it? Because there will be parts of the edge which are closer to the real edge and parts of the edge which are farther from the real edge. Any edge you can show me can be split to a finer edge.

Listen carefully. There is no edge around things. There is no edge where the blue meets the green. If you think carefully—go back over it later. The edge you think you see cannot be there; it's impossible. There's no edge where the land meets the water. There's no edge where the water starts up on to the land again. There's no edge where the foothills start. It can't be there. That's the first indication that what you think is there is not there, and it's not coming from what you thought it was coming from.

Then we spoke about how to see the future, what you will be, the beautiful thing you will become, and see it directly. We said, first you should have innocence; then you can start to believe, like a child.

"Does it really work? Did he tell us the right way?"

No, it doesn't work.

71

"Why?"

Many innocent people are hurt badly. There are many tragedies involving innocents.

Innocence doesn't lead to faith in seeing the glimmering of a great vision you will have later. Innocence doesn't have that power. Some innocent people see the beginning of truth. Some innocent people can see the beginning of a vision, which goes through all time and space. It is for them the beginning. But some innocent people just fail. So, innocence doesn't cause the beginning of this vision.
"But surely learning must help, the second step we talked about."

No, learning can't do anything. Many people learn and only get frustrated. Many others just get more proud. The learning hurts them; it makes them much worse than they were before. Learning doesn't have any power to help you to see every living creature and save them. Something deeper; there's a deeper power, there's a deeper energy.

"But surely questioning, debating, thinking must help. Surely contemplation must help bring the vision."

No. The process of debate, questioning, inquisition has turned many people rotten, proud, almost violent, competitive, jealous. Contemplation by itself has no power to give you this vision. Something deeper is underlying; there's a deeper seed.

"But surely meditation, sitting quietly in my little hut, focusing deeply and single-pointedly—this must be a way to see the future. This must be a way to break through the curtains, see all living beings. Everyone says this is a way to meet with holy beings, speak with them."

No. Many people meditate. They get frustrated; they get more angry than they were before. Many people sit for weeks or months thinking about someplace else, worrying about who might be thinking about them, the great meditator. Meditation doesn't have the power to bring you these visions, these direct insights, direct perceptions of the future. There's a deeper seed at work. That seed produces the visions; the deeper seed produces the ability to see what will come hundreds of years from now. There are people who can see hundreds of years away. There are people who can see what they will become, directly.

Some people will say, "That's wonderful. I didn't feel like doing all that work."

It's a very beautiful thing. The deep seed, the real seed will make you want to do the work. The seed that gives you the vision really, the eyes within your heart, which are ultimate eyes, that seed creates the learning; that seed creates the innocence; that seed creates the contemplation, and the meditation. And it always does that just before the vision. So, you have to do those things because you will do those things. You have to do those things because you will do those things, just before you see. That will be because of a deeper seed. Things don't change from unseen to seen. Things don't change from hidden to obvious. You don't go through any steps to go there. The steps don't even exist.

There's a beautiful path that goes from holy Lama Khen Rinpoche's driveway to his house. It was made by some of his dear students. You should look at it some time. It's just stones, flat stones. We are like people who have a handful of stones, and we've set them down one by one, and then we walk on them. They don't exist there in front of you.

When you go through the path, and you finally see what you will become, the future, and you meet holy beings, it's only stones that your mind is laying before your mind. Your mind lays down the darkness. Then your mind lays down the idea, "Maybe I could see the future." Then your mind lays down the two true images. And then your mind lays down the real thing. Your mind creates the future. Your mind creates every planet and every creature on it. Your mind creates holy beings, and then your mind serves it up to your mind. They are all only images.

"So you are saying that when I see the future, it will only be a picture in my mind?"

That's right.

"You are saying when I meet a holy being or my next-door neighbor now, this is only an image in my mind?"

Right.

"You are saying, when I heard you talk the last three days, I started to feel like I could do it. I felt like for the first time maybe someone could see the future directly, and see holy beings directly. Are you telling me you are only describing an image?"

That's right.

"So, they don't exist."

No, that's wrong. They are images, and that's *why* they exist.

"But if they are just images, then they are not real."

Go stand in front of a car, a fast car. See if the car breaks your legs. This is an image in your mind. A deep seed in your mind has created the image. And it hurts. "So who cares if it's an image if it works, like a real car hitting my legs. What's the point of telling me it's an image?"

We can have images that present themselves as images. If you haven't seen the future, and I say, "Imagine the future now, what you will become. Try to imagine what you will be in the end, a holy being," if you haven't seen that, then you start to make an image. But you know it's an image. And if I say, "Look at my hand now," you form an image, your mind forms an image. It's an image of an outside thing. And so it's an outside thing.

"Do outside things exist?"

No, only images.

"So there are no outside things."

Of course there are! They are the things which your mind forms as an image of an outside thing.
"Why are you telling us this? What's the difference? If it looks like an outside image, if my mind takes it that way, who cares?"

I'd like to introduce an old friend who is here. He was with us in New York during the classes, and he kindly came all around the world with us. Even in Mongolia, Ireland, other holy lands. I brought him. *[Laughter and clapping.]* He's the best emptiness teacher in the world. All over the world, people understood emptiness from him.

What is this thing? If you're smart, you'll say, "Red and white stick." If you're

74

new, you'll say, "No, that's a pen. Don't you guys see? It's a pen." *[Laughs.]*

[From child in audience: "Arf, arf."*]*

Wait, later.

Your eye only has the power to see shapes and colors. Your eye has no other power. Your eye can't see a pen. It takes a mental process to decide this is a pen. Your eye can only report to the brain, "We have a shape here," and the brain says, "What's it look like?" and the eye says, "Oh, it's a cylinder." Then the brain says, "What color is it?" and the eye says, "Oh the top is red and the bottom is white, and it's connected to five fat little sticks right now."

And the mind thinks it over, and says, "I bet he's holding up that stupid pen again."

So, it's the mind that makes this into a pen. The mind forms a picture of a pen. The mind forms the edges around it arbitrarily, based on a few clues. But, if this were a pen from its own side, and then if an animal from a different realm, a being from a different realm—the only other realm you and I can see now if you're a normal person, I don't know if there are any—is the animal realm.

So, if a dog ran in here and said, "Arf, arf, arf," and he looked up at this red and white stick, he wouldn't see a pen. He would probably just think, "Oh, maybe it's something to chew on; I'll try to get if from him later."

Your natural tendency, which is the source of all pain, is to think that because he's a dog, he sees something to chew on. That's not quite right. He's a dog *because* he sees something to chew on. He's a dog because he has deep seeds in his mind to see this otherwise neutral stick as something to chew on. And we are human because when we look at the same stick, we think it's something to write with.

Which one is it? The natural tendency is to say, "It's a pen, and the stupid dog is ruining my pen." And when you take it away, the dog says, "The stupid human is pulling away my chew thing again."

So who's right? They're both right. Each being's mind is forcing them to see something. That's the emptiness of this thing. It's not a pen from its own side. It's not something to chew on from its own side. Even when we see ourselves, even when we look down, even when we say something or do something, we see a person or we see a mind, because that person or that mind has been painted into the picture that we are painting. Nothing has any quality of its own. Nothing. Your body is not what it looks like from its own side. Your mind is forming that image.

Even your mind isn't what it feels like from its own side; your mind is making you feel your mind this way. The mind of the moment before, because of deep seeds, is making you hear your thoughts now. Everything is under the control of these deep seeds. Nothing has any nature of its own, nothing is anything by itself. It's the key to seeing what you will be. It's the key to seeing every living sweet creature there is on every world. It's the key to meeting holy angels.

If you find out the deep seed you need, you can do all of these things. I swear it. Because they don't exist from their own side.

We learned a special meditation. Before we take a break, I'd like to practice. We said learn to quietly, secretly, as you go through your day meeting with other people or sitting alone, sometimes close your eyes. Reach out to the right side; imagine that you could touch the first of a long line of living creatures in the whole universe, and you are comforting them. "I'm coming. I'm working very hard. Actually, I'm very close, and I know it."

Then sometimes reach behind you. Imagine that the sweet, holy teacher, your main teacher from your last life, is touching your hand.

Now, a third meditation added tonight. You know the way. You sit in front of your altar or on your airplane, and say quietly but out loud, "When I make this special motion to my left, it means I'm trying to touch one of the holy angels who are around me that I cannot see now." They have two parts: one is that beautiful self-making-love body of light we talked about. But their core, their essence, the quality which enables them to be on every world at once, is the same emptiness that this stick has. So imagine it, try to touch them. Try to feel. Think about their body, or think about their core. And then someday that seed will grow in your mind: you will see them, you will talk to them. You will see their real nature; it will change you forever.

Then reach out your hand to the front and get some refreshments. And then come back, and we will really finish quickly after that.

[Break]

We said that your mind was painting your world like a workman laying down stones of a path and then walking on them. The mind creates an image and then serves it up to the mind. But the mind is helpless; the mind is in powerful hands; the mind can only do what it's told to do; the mind can only paint what it's told to paint. We don't have a choice in the present moment.

There are deeper seeds. Those seeds absolutely dictate everything around us, and even how our minds sound and think. Try to understand. This is a stick. If you have seeds in your mind, you will see it as a pen, and you will grasp deeply, hard. Your heart will insist that this is a pen. It's hard to even imagine how it looks like to a dog. It's hard to admit that what the dog sees is just as real.

This is not a pen. And it's not something to chew on. It's only what those deep seeds make you see. Try to understand what I say next. The quality of being into the future, the quality of being something already past, is exactly the same. You have ceased to be split into three times. We have seeds to be limited to a present moment. We have seeds to perceive time in a linear, sequential fashion. We have seeds to divide all time into the future, which we are blind to—deadly blindness. We have seeds to forget the past, and not even be able to see what we were. And we have seeds to be stuck in a single instant of infinite time.

These are only images. These are only images thrown up to your mind by seeds in your mind. Time doesn't have to be that way. Time is not self-existent. Time doesn't exist from its own side any more than pens do. Holy beings don't have a word for past, future, present. They just see everything now. And the seeds in their mind force them to see it. Try to understand what I say. There's no far or near. Being here, being close to here, and being far from here are only images that your mind forces you to see, like the image of a pen. They don't exist. Far, near, and here don't exist. We have seeds in our minds which force us to see these divisions. They don't exist. If we could identify the way to make strong enough seeds, we wouldn't have to live in a box and die like that. Your mind will come to see all time. Your mind will come to see all the places there are in every moment that you live. You can save people. We have a choice. We can either die in this little box called "now," a moment, or we can live forever with beautiful holy beings, and we can see and travel to the places where suffering people need us who are stuck in their own boxes.

We have all this capability; we have all this capacity because things are empty. Things are produced by seeds in your mind. It's true that a pen feels and writes like a pen whether it's really outside or whether it's an image. It's no different. But if you know it's an image, then you can change it. You can plant new seeds in your mind, powerful seeds. This is what all of us have to do. The choice is death. The choice is letting down all the countless beings in *your* world, who are waiting for you. They are waiting for you. Each person here will save the people in their world. Stop thinking it's someone else; it's you.

"How do I plant the seeds?"

There's only one seed. There's only one thing that will make your meditation work. There's only one thing that will make your learning work. It's the seed underneath all other seeds. It's kindness, being kind to other people. We are stuck in a box called the present moment. We are almost crippled, blind. We can't see anything that's important, because our kindness is so small.

I'm not being poetic. I'm not speaking in metaphors. I'm not trying to give you some warm fuzzy feeling. This is a difference between death and life with holy beings. Our kindness is too small. It plants seeds in our mind that make us small.

I watch the ants. They come to a huge stone near our porch. It's huge because it's kind of high for them; it's two feet high maybe. And they walk into the stone about an eighth of an inch from the edge. And they climb over the stone rather than walking around. They struggle desperately up two feet and then desperately down two feet—four feet, when they could walk around an eighth of an inch. They couldn't see. Holy beings look at us sadly in the same way. We can't see. The people who would help us to see are like ants who get up to lecture the other ants. "Come on, guys, you could just walk around the rock."

"I don't know what you're talking about. We just go over."

"How kind do I have to be to see those things? I really want to see those things. I get a sense from your voice that it's possible."

How big is your kindness? Where is the edge of your kindness?

Some people, and me—I feel like that sometimes—they have a strange kindness; it only goes halfway down their body. They take care of the mouth. They stuff the mouth with nice sweet things. They are kind to the mouth, and then it hurts the rest of the body. The edge of their kindness only goes to their throat. They will eat something which is kind to their mouth and hurts the rest of their body.

People who smoke have a similar kind of kindness. They are kind to their throats or their mouths, and they are killing the rest. The edge or the line of their kindness only goes down to their throat. There are other people whose kindness only goes as far as their sexual organ. To please the organ, to please a few inches of their body, they will risk the life of the rest of the body. They will risk a disease that has no cure for a few moments of kindness to their organ. They will destroy the body that holds the organ. Their kindness only goes a few inches on their bag of skin.

Then there are many people whose kindness goes to the whole bag of skin. They are kind to their own bag of skin. They clothe and feed their own bag of skin, they wash their own bag of skin with special love and attention, and other bags of skin should try to work it out the best they can. "I don't care. I want the best for my bag of skin. My bag of skin should have pretty clothes; my bag of skin's hair should be washed nicely."

Some people stretch the edge of their kindness further. They take a wife, or a husband, or a boyfriend or a girlfriend. And because the two bags of skin can stay together and keep warm, or because the two bags of skin eat in the same room, then their kindness will stretch to both bags of skin. My husband or wife should have the best. And similar with other relatives.

Then other people's kindness will go further, to the bag of skin that came out of their bag of skin. "This is my child. This bag of skin came from my bag of skin. This child is special; this child needs attention; this child needs better things."
In the scripture, a mother's love is given as the most powerful. But it can be a very selfish thing, if the edge of the kindness only goes to their own children. It can be one of the saddest things in the world.

"Are you telling me if the child next door were being beaten, if the child next door were being abused, you wouldn't do something? If their bag of skin didn't come out of your bag of skin?"

They will answer, "What do you think I am, an animal? Of course I would do something. I would go next door. I would talk to the parents. I would try to help."

79

"And if a bag of skin were traveling in a car in front of your house, and if that car hit another car and that bag of skin went through the windshield and was bleeding, and you could help, would you help that bag of skin?"

"Of course I would. I'm not crazy! If I could help them, if I could stop the bleeding, if I were trained to help others, of course I would help them."

"And if the accident took place on the next street over in your neighborhood, would you run and help? If everyone was depending on you, waiting for you, if the person was bleeding enough? Even if their bag of skin was different, even if their bag of skin was farther away, would you run?"

"Of course I would run."

"And if there was a child next door who was hungry, didn't have enough food, would you put some of your food in that bag of skin, or would you continue to overfeed the bags of skin in your own house?"

"Of course I would share my food."

"And if the child were on the next street or across town, would you go and give them food?"

"I guess so, how far?"

"What if in another town? What if in another state? What if they lived on the other side of the world? How far does your kindness go?"

"I don't know about the other side of the world thing. They are pretty far away."

These are the days of the internet; these are the days of CNN. I can give you the names of children who are hungry in Sera Monastery. I can give you the names of holy monk teachers who have tuberculosis from not enough food. You can send your extra money. Talk to John Brady. He's here. Geshe Ngawang Rigdol can give it to them. It takes five minutes.

We're not in a big world anymore. We are in a small world. You can't ignore. Your kindness has to be bigger. They are as good as next door. You can't forget

80

them. You can't pretend they are not hungry anymore. You can't go on being kind to two or three bags of skin and ignore the others. You will never see anything, because the karma, the seed you plant when you are kind to one or two bags of skin is very cruel. You will die in that bag of skin. It will always be that small. You will never see the things that are important. You can't see them now because of, *because of*, the lie of the bags of skin.

"What about the children in Africa?"

"Oh, they are very different."

"Oh, there are towns and cities where half the people are dying of AIDS. You know it."

"But they are very different. They don't speak a language at all like mine."

"How different is different? If the person who is dying in a car accident in front of your house looks different, will you ignore them? If they speak a different language, will you ignore them? If your own bag of skin produced a bag of skin that only had one arm or one leg, would you ignore it because it looked different?"

"No of course I would take care of it."

"Then why do you ignore the bags of skin with four legs?"

"They are different than me."

"How different do they have to be? Where is the edge of your kindness? Where does it stop?"

"Oh, if they have four legs, but they are cuddly, if they lick my face when I feed them, then my kindness will go that far."

"What if they're big and ugly and fat and moo all the time? Will your kindness go to them too, or will you kill them for their skin?

Will you take care of a baby?"

81

"Of course I'll take care of a baby."
"No, you shouldn't. They're small."

"That doesn't matter. Small doesn't matter. It can feel; it has feelings."

"Then take care of the other small creatures."

"How small?"

"How about mice?"

"OK, but no smaller."

"How about insects?"

"They are too different. They are too small. They don't speak my language at all."

If you live in the desert with the animals, you will see something. We—Christie and I—were sitting on the porch. We set out your lovely cookies for them, and they eat throughout the day. They sneak under the fence where we left a big hole on purpose, and in the gate, and they come all day. We noticed something strange, very strange. They started to come only when we are sitting on the porch. We only sit on the porch for a few minutes a day; they seem to be waiting. There's a rabbit; there's a coyote; there are many birds. They could eat all day long, but they come to eat when we are there.

It struck me one day, this beautiful rabbit. He would eat the cookies, and then the grass, in miles of grass. And then I realized, he's lonely; he's just lonely, and he's afraid. And the coyote is lonely, and he's afraid. Outside of the fence, it's just killing. They go to their homes at night. There's a squirrel who came and ripped all the cushions off our chair, and stuffed it in her house in the ground for her children. They have homes. They go to bed at night. They get lonely. They appreciate some nice chocolate chip cookies. They are just like us. So, why not be kind to them? Why do you put an edge to your kindness? That border of your kindness is your death. That border, the limit of your kindness is the limit of your vision. It creates the seeds, which make us blind.

Those people, the holy people that I mentioned: Moses, Jesus, Lord Buddha, the early Indian saints, the great lamas of Tibet, they overcame their blindness. They saw holy beings, holy places, because they were kind to everything, and that kindness put a seed in their mind that destroyed the curtain. It destroyed the edges of the little box we live in. I'm not being poetic; I'm not being nice; this is just true.

"So if you open up your refrigerator and there are two donuts there to eat, and you can't get to the store tomorrow, would you leave one for tomorrow or not? How far does your kindness go into the future?"

"I would leave one, if I wasn't feeling kind of like eating both of them, because tomorrow's me will want one."

So, your kindness can go into the future. The edge of your kindness has to go far, even into the future. We have a problem in our country. We are kind to the current generation at the expense of future generations. We know we are using up things too fast, we know we are making our earth dirty, but our kindness is not big enough to go into the future. We can't be kind to people we have never met. We can't be kind to people who aren't born yet.

And I tell you that there are worlds that you can't see. There are realms all around us; you can see them one day. One day in a single minute or two of absolute inner vision clarity, with your eyes that are in your heart, you will see every world there is. You will see every living being who lives on them. You have to take care of them too.

"Are you telling me my kindness has to extend to some imaginary planets you are talking about that I can't even see and that no one around me has ever seen? Are you telling me if my kindness doesn't reach to people who haven't been born, or who may not be born for ten or ten thousand years, are you telling me it's my responsibility to learn to be kind to them also?"

It's like the disciple who turned to Jesus and said, "You expect me to take care of all my brothers' needs also? You expect me to give him all my food? You expect me to worry about what he's going to wear? You expect me to take care of everything this other person needs?"

And Jesus said, "Of course!"

It's what you're here for. It's the only thing we are supposed to do. We have to take care of all the beings we can see, and we have to take care of all the beings we can't see. We have to take care of all of the beings around us now, and our kindness has to go ahead in the future to all of the people who come. It's what you're here for. Your heart knows it. I'm not telling you something you don't know; we just kind of forget sometimes.

"So, what will happen if my kindness gets this big? No limit, no edge."

"*Tseme shi,* the four immeasurables, it means the four edgelesses. Then the seeds in your mind will be perfect."

"Do you expect me to feed all the people in India or in Africa?"

"No, you can't; I'm not talking about that. It's a big difference between wanting to and doing it. Lord Buddha couldn't do it. Jesus couldn't do it. But they were perfect. Why? Because they wanted to and they were willing to, and they gave everything they could give. That's enough."

"What will happen to me if I do what you say? What will happen to me if my kindness goes beyond my own bag of skin and the bags of skin that live in my house?"

"You will become the savior of countless beings. You will become like the Jesus of your own world. I swear you will. It's what you want to do; it's what you were meant to do. You are going to do it now."

"How long will it take?"

"Not long; you are very close."

The wind is blowing hard here; why do you think? The winds inside you are coming close. They are running; they didn't run before.

"Oh, don't be superstitious. It's just the wind."

"The wind is an image. The image of the wind is created by the winds inside of you. The energy of man and woman, the other holy energies in all of you are coming together. You are very close. The wind is blowing in honor of you."

84

Last meditation: There will come a day when you will see ahead; you will see yourself as you will be. It's a joy. Imagine seeing yourself being the Jesus, or the Buddha, or the Moses of your people, of your whole world, of many worlds. You will be. It's not crazy or prideful to think it. It's your destiny, and it's a joy. One day you will see ahead and you will see yourself.

Something very beautiful: yourself as you will be—if you are not already—is watching you now. Yourself as you will become, the savior of countless creatures, is watching you now. Time doesn't matter to him or her.

So sometimes when you remember this last talk and these last words, then put your hand out to the front. And yourself will look upon you and be very happy, "Oh I remember, that was when I first believed what I would become."

When your future self is watching you now, put out your hand. And he or she or them are very happy. They are always watching you and waiting. They know what you are going to be. So reach out to them sometimes. Make a secret sign. You can do it all day. It's a very beautiful way to live.

That's all I have to say. Please make your kindness as big as you can. And on behalf of all the people in retreat, and the caretakers, holy people, and the other people working so hard here and in other places, New York, we are extremely grateful to you. We can't begin to pay you back.

Verses:

I.

We can see the sky.
Blue, lit from within;
Better than any sapphire.

We can see the stars,
Fire itself,
Beyond any diamond.

We can see the mountains
And hold the warmth of earth in our hands.

We can see life,
Sparks of intelligence and kindness:
We can see each other.

Down our streets we can see
Schools, hospitals,
Homes for the elderly,

Churches and people of every kind;
Peace,
Striving to reach and touch -

This precious, present moment.

A pinpoint
On an unseen plain
That knows no horizon.

A pinpoint
In an unseen river

That stretches forever.

It is
Too much not to see.
It is
Where have we come from?
What will become of us?
What have we come here to do?

It is
All the only things
That matter.

To see
You have to have a reason
To see; it is
The one thing left unseen
Because we do not want
To see it.

Children of the rabbit
In the dark of a thousand
Miles of empty desert,

Caught in the jaws of the serpent;
Who will help us?

You know us.

For better or worse,
We have worked
Side by side.

You see our houses;
You know where we live,
You know what we try to do.

II.

Stumbling to our graves
In boxes
A little bigger than ourselves;
Cloaked in four silver curtains
At the edge of what we see.

Ahead, what we will be;
Behind, what we were.

On the right side
Endless worlds
And the hearts of those who wait
In pain and hope for us.

On the left,
Beings of the divine,
Themselves a higher truth.

Draw them to you;
Call them first
From the dark world of *Viparyaya*,
The realm of cannot be.

Next through the mists
Of the ocean of *Vikalpa*,
Place of the maybe could.
And then the first great leap,

To the sturdy shores of *Agama*,
First land of it is,
A deeply hidden is,
For spoken it was so.

Closer, to the highlands
Of *Anumana*:
The simply hidden is,

At reason's true demand.

Then lastly to the sunlit peaks
Of the mountains of *Pratyaksha*
Second great leap, the undeniable power
Of something in your hand.

To remember,
Think of the vegetables,
And remember reaching out to touch.
Their hands just there, to the right.

III.

Leave the dark world
On the ship of openness,
Hope, and innocence.

Cross to the highlands
On the steed of learning;
Use the staff of contemplation
To come to the base of the peaks.

The mountains can only be scaled
With the rope of meditation;
The sun of the Beings of Light
Shines upon them all.

Tu sam gom sum:
The ways of wisdom are old
And have not aged a day.

First find a Guide who knows the way
Both by head and foot;
The hour to hour, and a friend.

Then take yourself to the classics;
A voice in a thousand years.
Commit the directions to memory
The song within your head,
A companion for you and others
Whenever you need; select.

Walk; take small and steady steps
Circle thrice, then once for meaning
At the end half again, for firmness.

Sing along beads, watch for holes,
Return at times, use your time.
Be graceful when it flies;

IV.

Throughout history,
Only the very good
Have seen.
Why?

Because there is nothing seen,
And there is nothing unseen.
There is no dark world,
There are no mists,
No shore, no highlands, no peaks:
The edges are impossible

No innocence,
Nothing to learn,
Nothing to contemplate,
Nothing on which to meditate.
The seed grows the flower
And the plant tags along.

Nothing is hidden,
Nothing revealed;
And you cross from one to the other
By sitting very still—
The mountain comes to you.

For we are workmen
Laying down path stones,
Then walking on them:
We lay down the dark,
We lay down the dim image,
We lay down the two true images,
And we lay down the solid object.

Our minds organize an image
Of an image as an image;

91

And our minds organize an image
Of an object as an object.
Don't confuse the two,
And don't think they're not real.

We are painters,
Painting each scene,
Then stepping into it
As we paint ourselves there.

It was never any other way;
This itself is Their very care.
Reach out to the left
To the light of a Diamond Sun.

Know though
That powerful hands move our own;
One thing decides pen or stick to chew on,
One thing decides the far and here,
The long away or now,
Lonely death or the company of Angels,
And that is kindness.

How kind? What edge?
How far from tongue to stomach?
How far too far?
How different too different?
How long ahead too long?

Do you expect me to feel responsible for people on worlds
that neither I nor others have ever seen; for those
who won't even be born for ten months or ten years
or ten thousand years?
Yes, it's what you are here to do;
And they are not unseen, nor unborn.
Reach ahead to the one who sees you,
Reach out to yourself.

Acknowledgements

A big thank you to all the people who helped make the three-year retreat and these teachings happen.

To the retreatants Geshe Michael Roach, Lama Christie McNally, Lama Thubten Pelma, Lama Trisangma Watson, Lama Ora Maimes, and Ven Tenzin Chogkyi, thank you for inspiring us all and dedicating your lives to serve others.

It could not have happened without the caretakers. Thank you to Ven. Jigme Palmo (Elly van der Pas), Amber Moore and Ven Lobsang Chukyi (Anne Lindsey); Brian Pearson, Sarah Laitinen, Sid Johnson, Keith Nevin, Ven. Gyelse (Gail Deutsch), Mercedes Bahleda, and Deb Bye, who helped with everything.

And to Winston and Andrea McCullough, the directors of Diamond Mountain, and their wonderful children; Ted and Andrea Lemon, who shared their home; David and Susan Stumpf and everyone else who helped with construction; the 400 sponsors who helped pay the bills, and the 187 people who came to the teachings; our lamas and teachers Khen Rinpoche Geshe Lobsang Tharchin, Geshe Thubten Rinchen, Lama Zopa Rinpoche, Sir Gene Smith, Sharon Gannon, David Life, David Swenson, Lady Ruth Lauer, and Laura Donnelly; Jerry and Marjorie Dixon, who let us use their land; John Brady, John Stillwell, Salim Lee, and the many many secret angels, (you know who you are) who keep pretending that you are normal people.

The Quiet Retreat Teaching books were brought into the world by the work of many hands. Ven. Jigme Palmo of Diamond Mountain University Press morphed the teachings into book form. Special thanks for layout and cover design to Katey Fetchenhier. DMU-Press intern Michelle Ross was a huge help with printing logistics. Thank you for endless hours of proof-reading to Joel Crawford, Michela Wilson, Kelly Fetchenhier, Janice Sanders, Karlie Sanders, Cassie Heinle, Lindsay Nelson, and Michelle Ross. Big thank you to Marc Ross for spending his precious free hours making manuscript corrections. We would especially like to express boundless appreciation to Ven. Jigme Palmo for her uncanny ability to do 10 things at once—and do them all well.

And of course, our infinite gratitude to our Teacher, Geshe Michael Roach, without whom these extraordinary teachings would not exist.

CPSIA information can be obtained
at www.ICGtesting.com
Printed in the USA
LVHW011642070820
662641LV00002B/372

9 780983 747833